A-Z Street Atlas of
READING

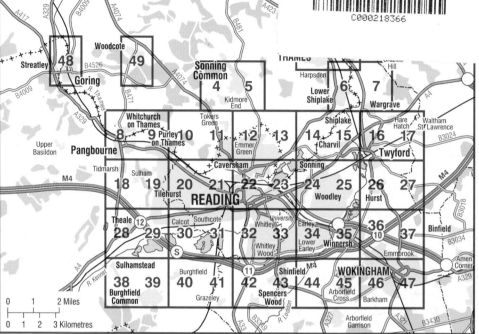

Reference

Motorway **M4**	Track `=======`	Car Park Selected **P**
A Road **A329**	Footpath `-------`	Church or Chapel **†**
Under Construction	Residential Walkway `··········`	Fire Station **■**
Proposed	Railway — Level Crossing / Station	Hospital **Ⓗ**
B Road **B3270**	Built Up Area (MILL / ST.)	House Numbers A & B Roads only **113 / 98**
Dual Carriageway	Local Authority Boundary `— ·· — ·· —`	Information Centre **ℹ**
		National Grid Reference ¹45
One Way Street	Posttown Boundary `———`	Police Station **▲**
Traffic flow on A Roads is indicated by a heavy line on the drivers left.	Postcode Boundary Within Posttown `— — —`	Post Office **★**
Pedestrianized Road `I======I`		Toilet **▽**
Restricted Access `⟦======⟧`	Map Continuation **▲ 10**	Toilet With Facilities for the Disabled **♿**

Scale

1:15,840
4 inches to 1 mile

0 — ¼ — ½ — ¾ mile

0 — 250 — 500 — 750 — 1 kilometre

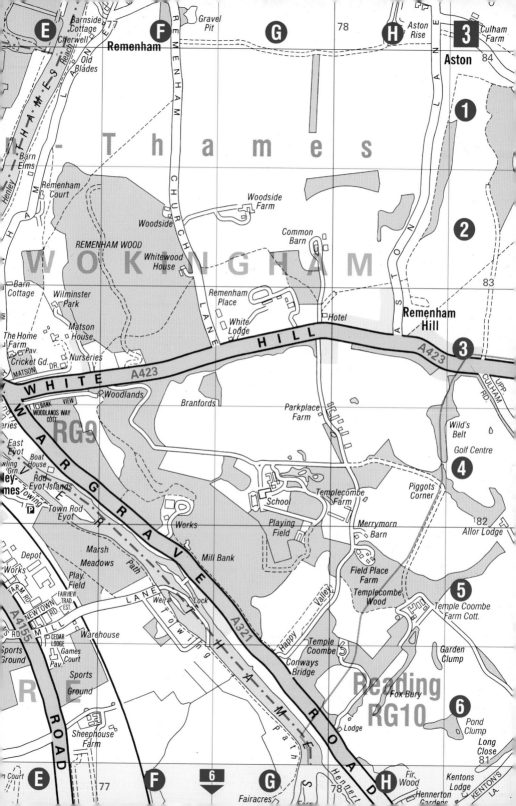

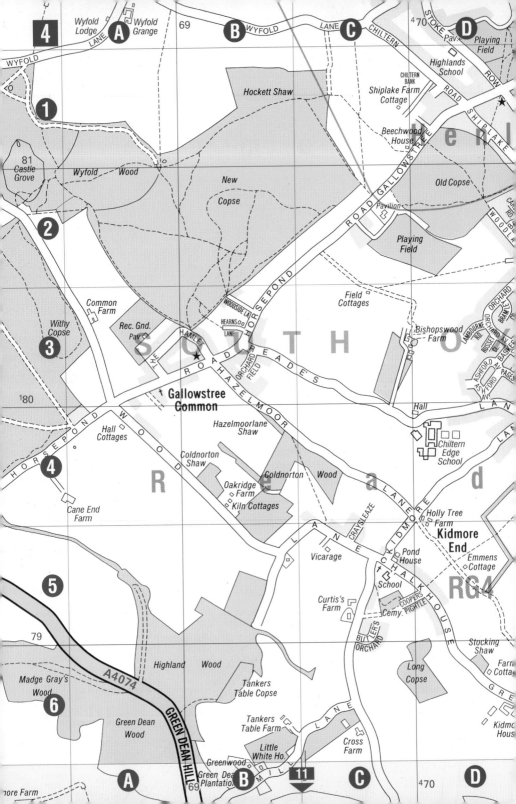

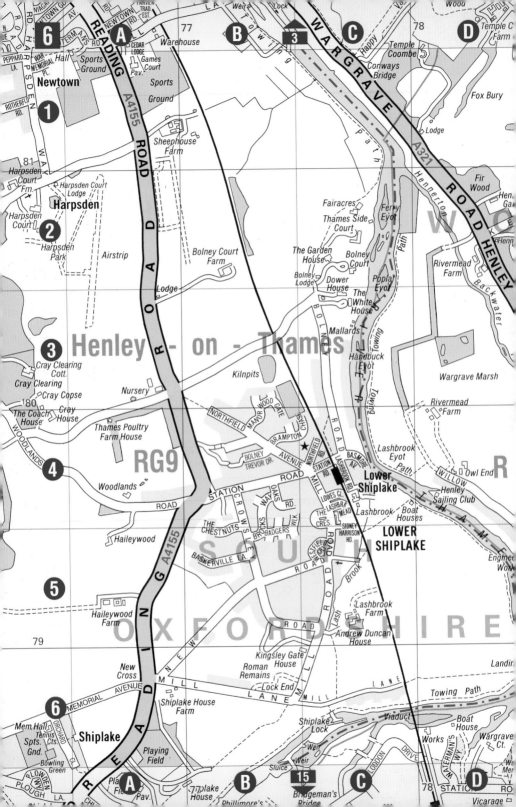

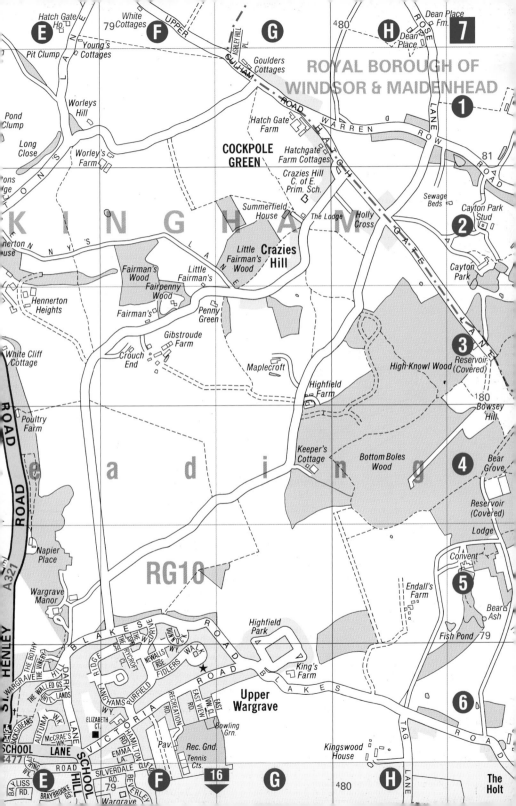

E Hatch Gate Ho.
79 White Cottages **F**
UPPER
G
H Dean Place Fm.
Dean Place
7

Young's Cottages
ASHLEY HILL PL.
Goulders Cottages
ROYAL BOROUGH OF
WINDSOR & MAIDENHEAD
480
ROSE
1

Pit Clump
Worleys Hill
WILHAM
ROAD
WARREN
LANE
ROW

Pond Clump
Hatch Gate Farm
HATCH
81

Long Close
Worley's Farm
COCKPOLE GREEN
Hatchgate Farm Cottages
Crazies Hill C. of E. Prim. Sch.
GATE
Sewage Beds
2 Cayton Park Stud

K I N G H A M
NNY'S
LANE
Summerfield House
CRAZIES HILL
The Lodge
Holly Cross
Cayton Park

Little Fairman's Wood
Little Fairman's
LANE
High Knowl Wood
3 Reservoir (Covered)
180
Bowsey Hill

Fairman's Wood
Fairpenny Wood
Fairman's
Penny Green
Gibstroude Farm
Maplecroft
Highfield Farm

Hennerton Heights
Crouch End
White Cliff Cottage
e a d i n g
Keeper's Cottage
Bottom Boles Wood
4 Bear Grove

Poultry Farm
Reservoir (Covered)
Lodge

Napier Place
RG10
Convent
5 Endall's Farm
Bear Ash

Wargrave Manor
A321
ROAD
ROAD
HENLEY ST. WARGRAVE
BLAKES
Highfield Park
Highfield Park
King's Farm
Fish Pond 79

THE VINERY
THE BOTHY
PARK LANE
THE WALLED GS
LANDS
RIDGE
LANGHAMS WY
PURFIELD
THE RISE
RYCROFT
DUNLOCK WY
NEWALLS
THE RISE CL.
FIDLERS
WALK
ROAD
Upper Wargrave
LAKES
6

AUTUMN WK
BLACKSDEANS WK
McCRAE'S WK
ELIZABETH CT.
VICTORIA
HAMILTON CL.
EMMA LA.
RECREATION RD.
EAST VIEW
EAST RD.
JW. CL.
VIW. CL.
Bowling Grn.
Kingswood House
TAG ROAD

SCHOOL
477
LANE
SCHOOL HILL
ROAD
SILVERDALE RD.
BEVERLEY CL.
Pav.
Rec. Gnd.
Tennis Cts.
480
E
LISS RD.
BRAYBROOKE GS
Wargrave
79
F
16
G
H
LANE
The Holt

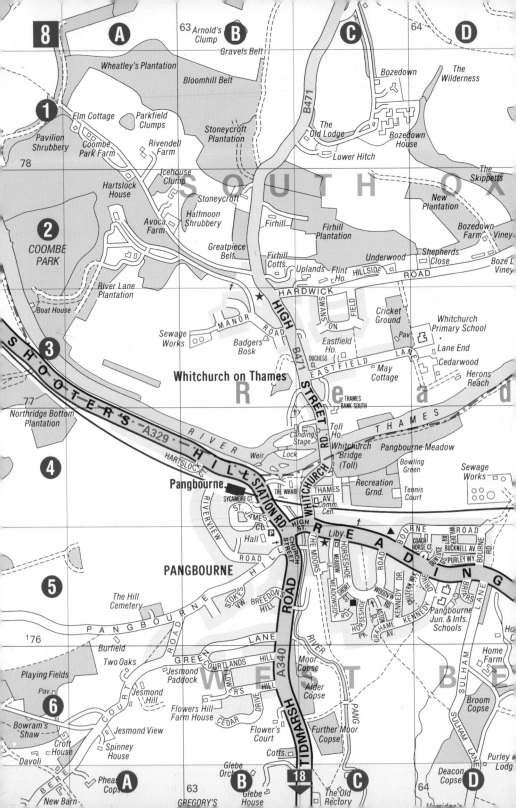

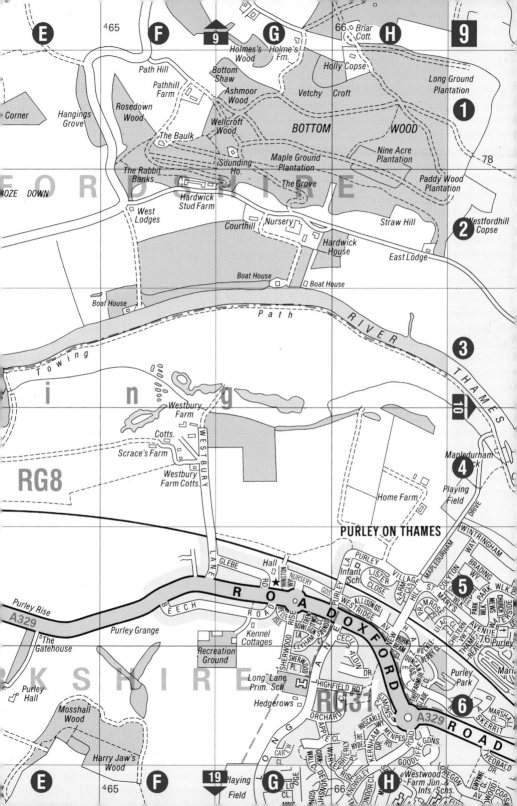

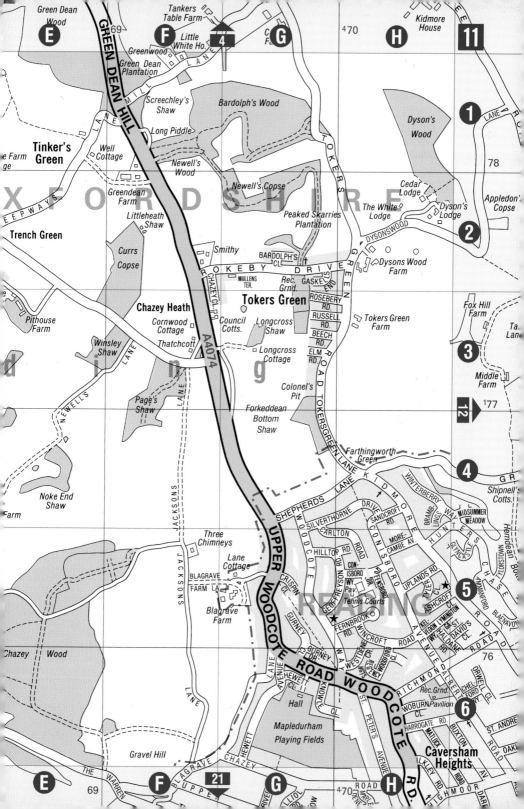

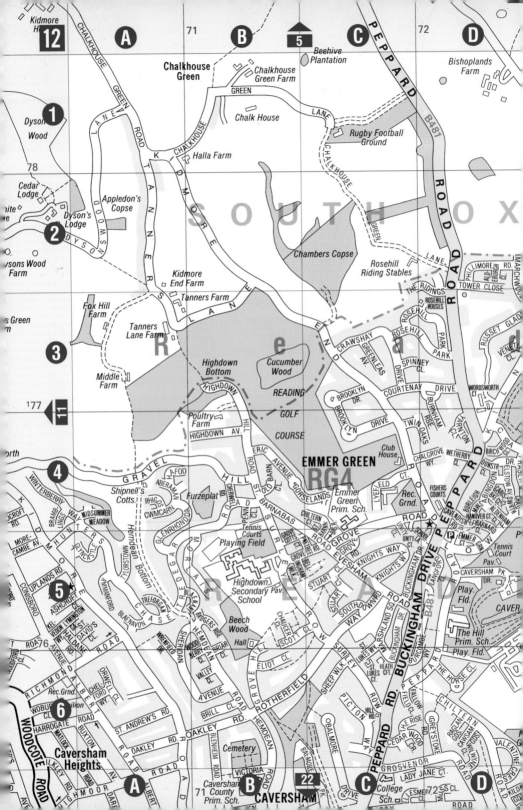

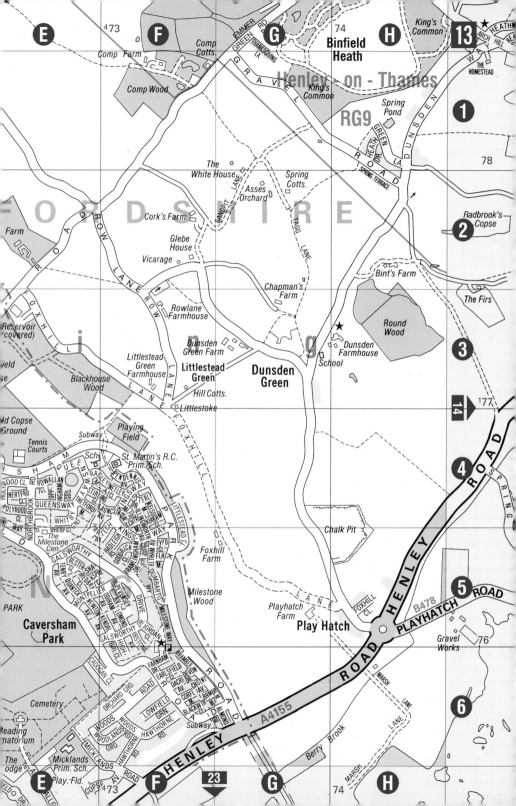

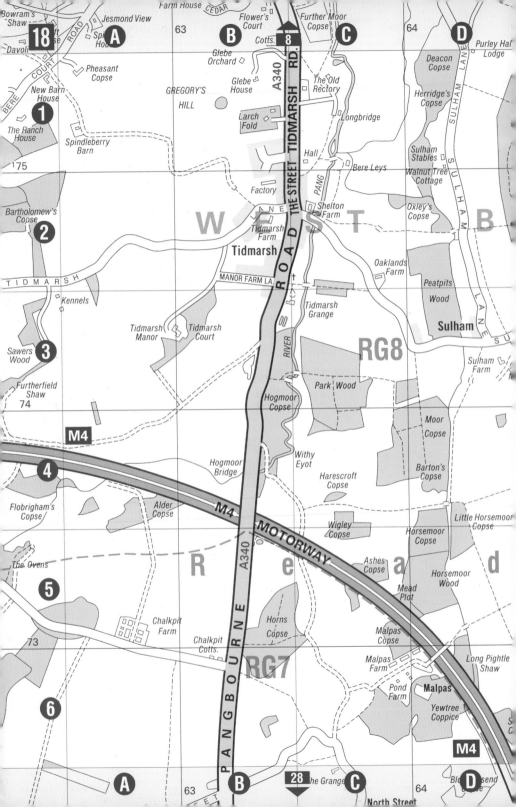

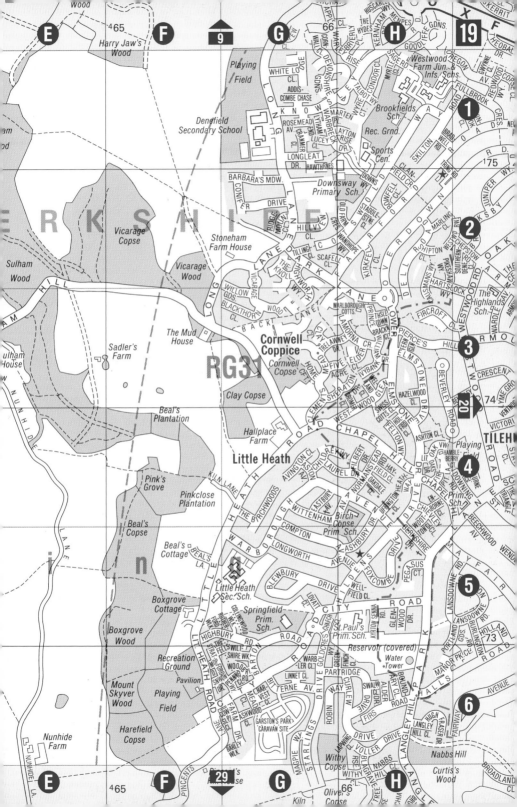

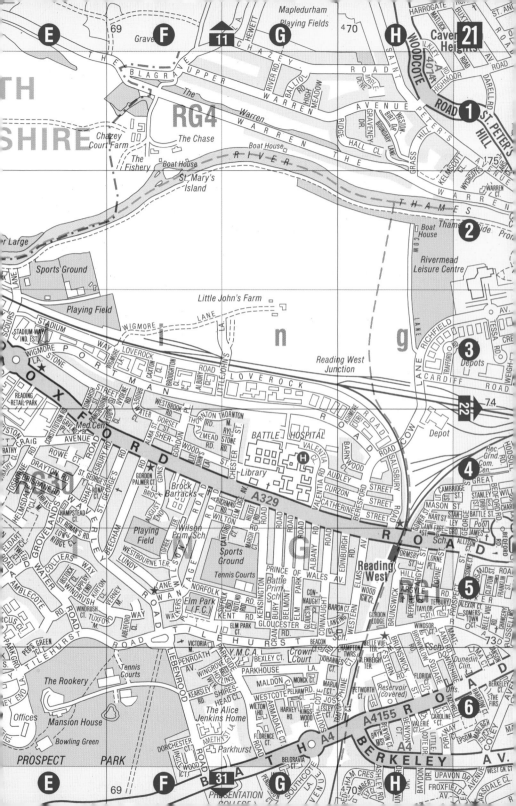

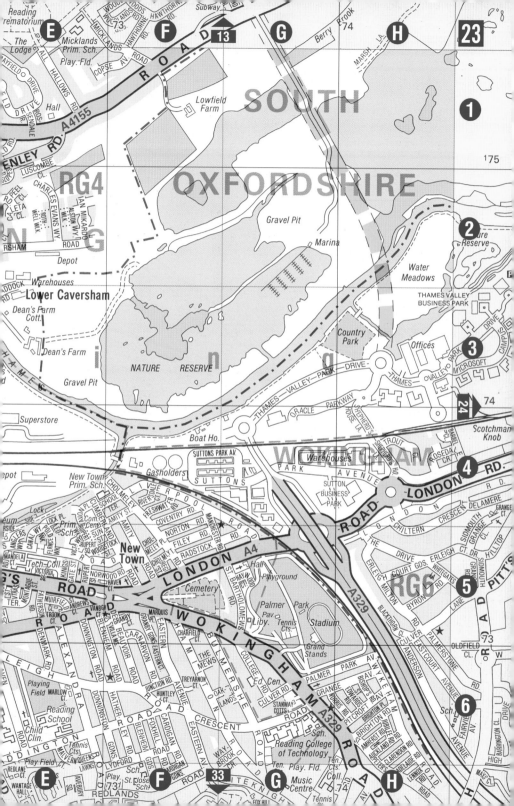

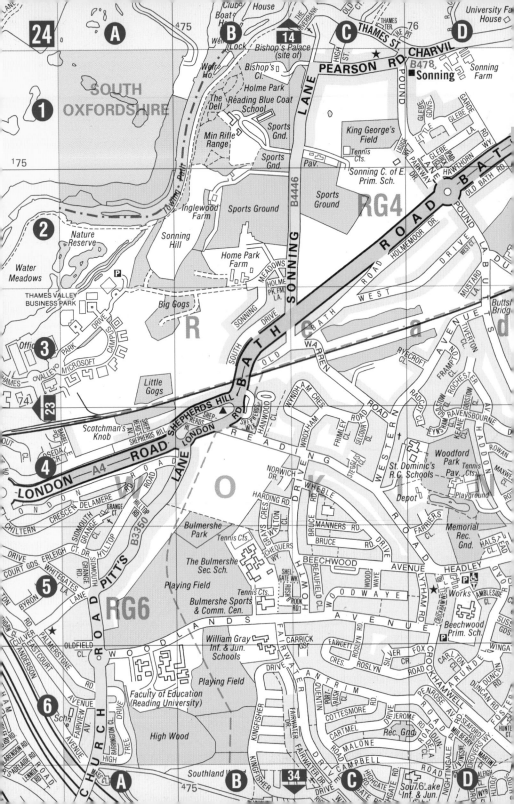

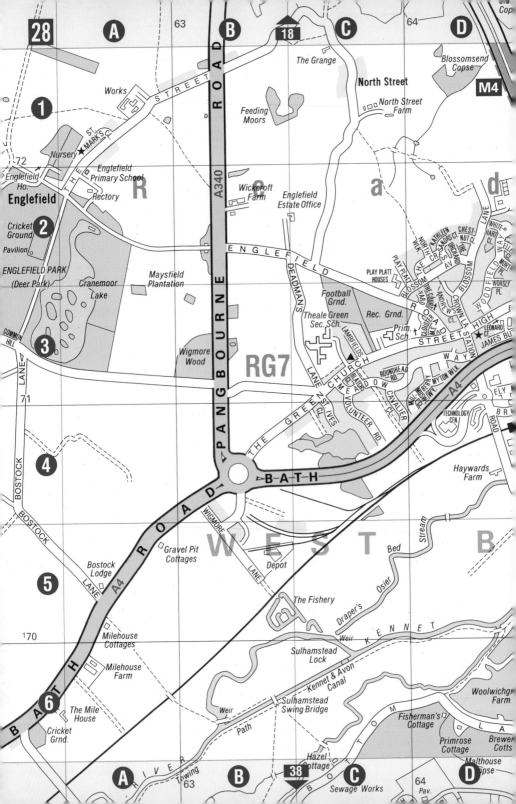

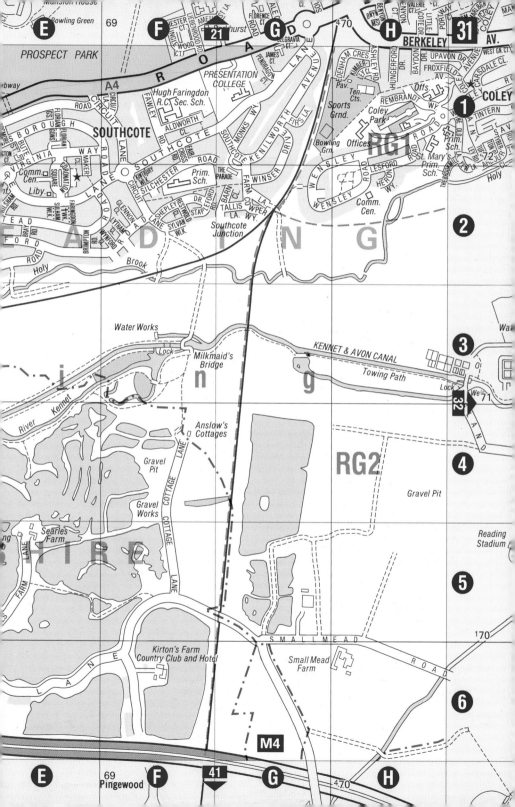

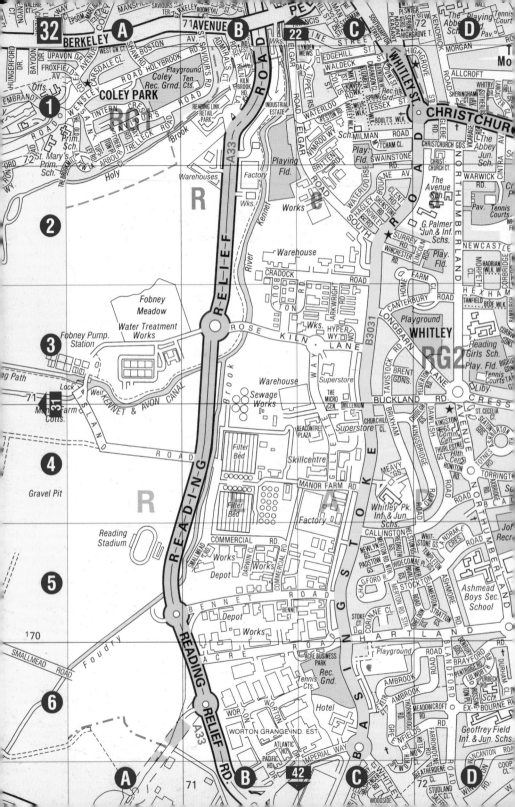

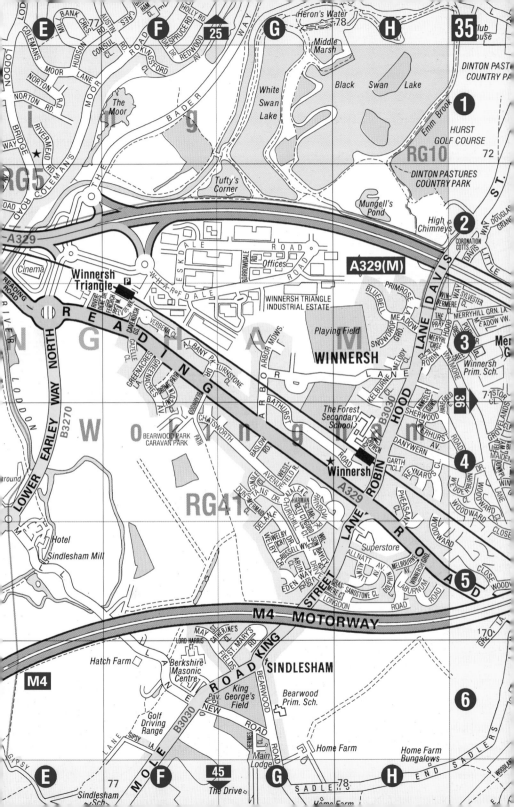

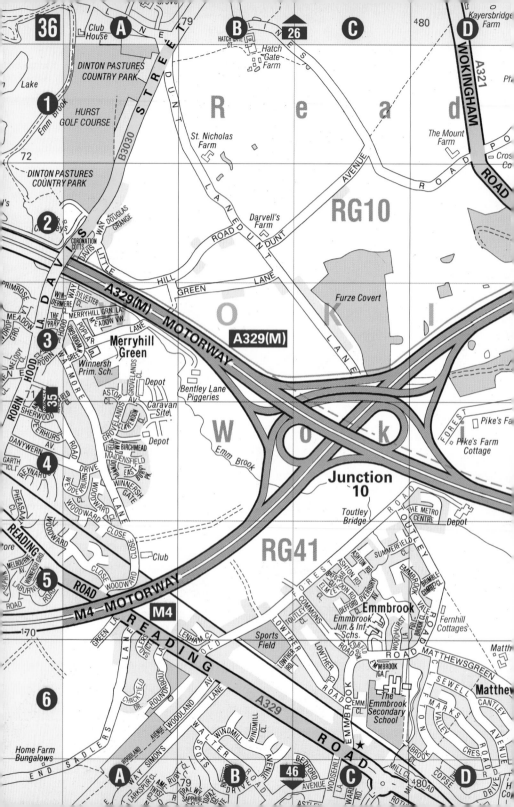

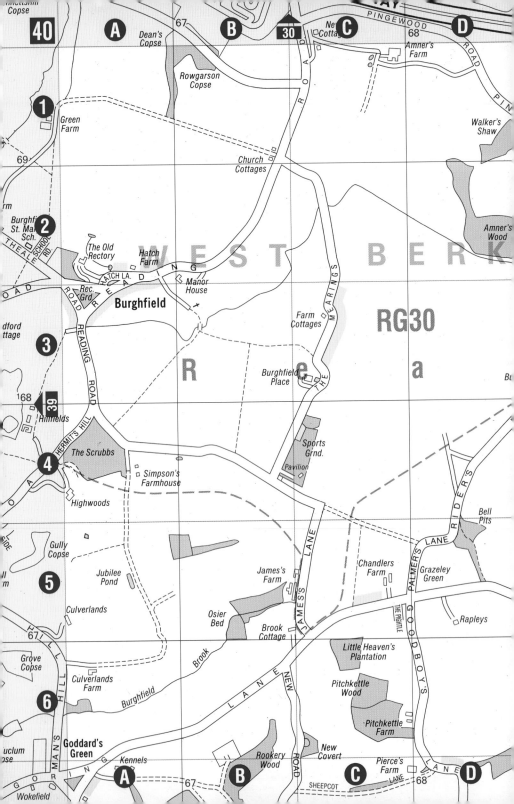

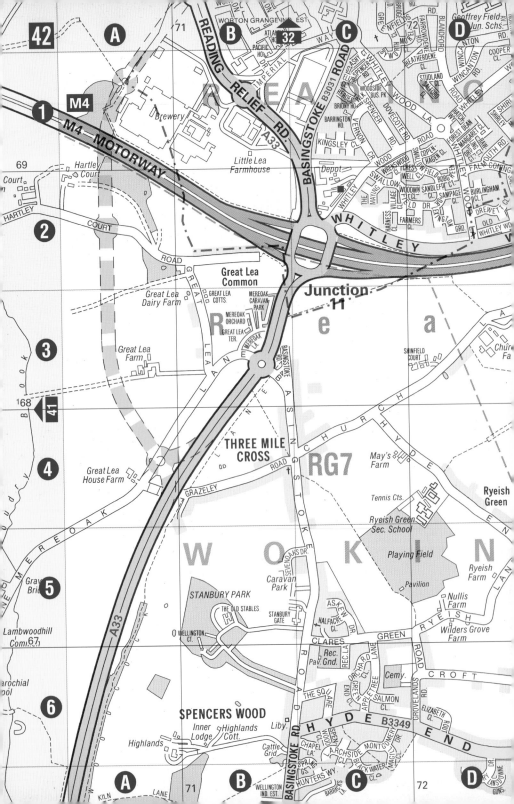

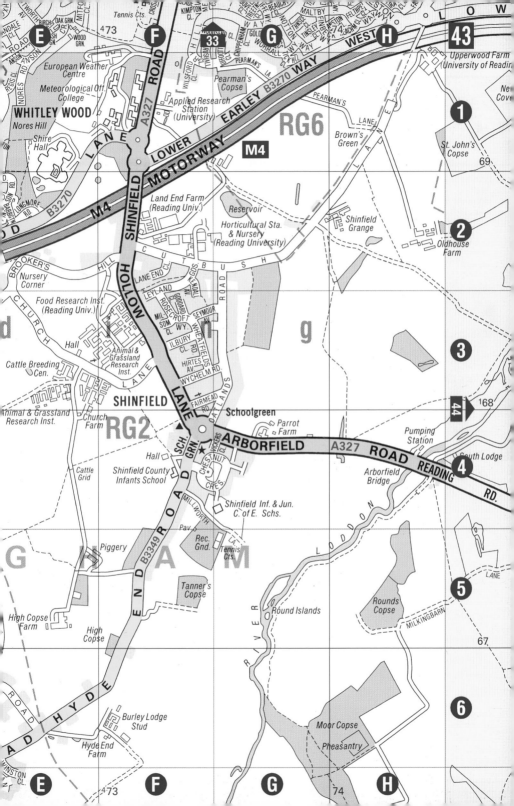

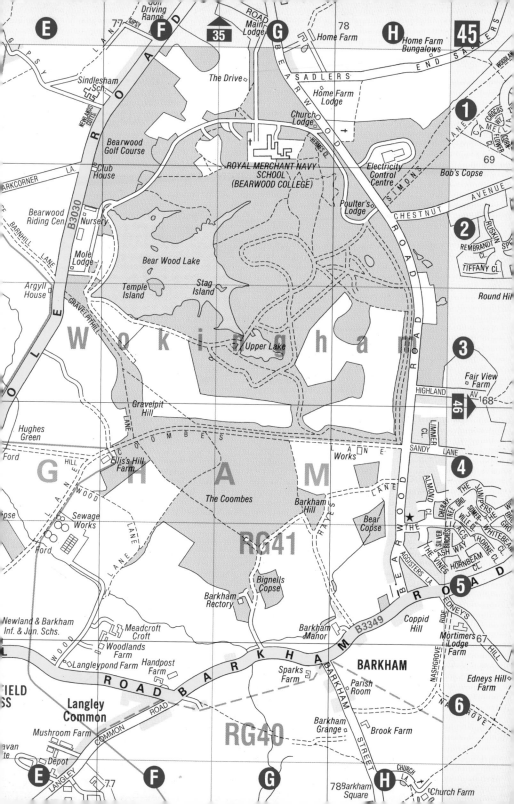

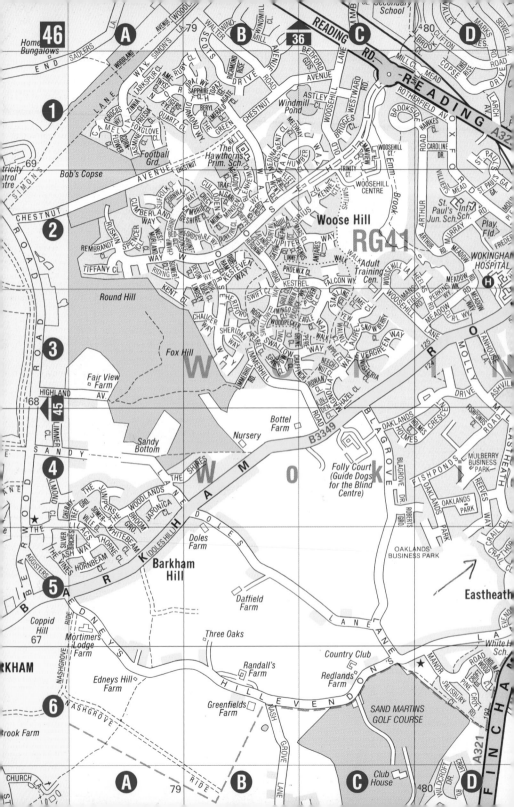

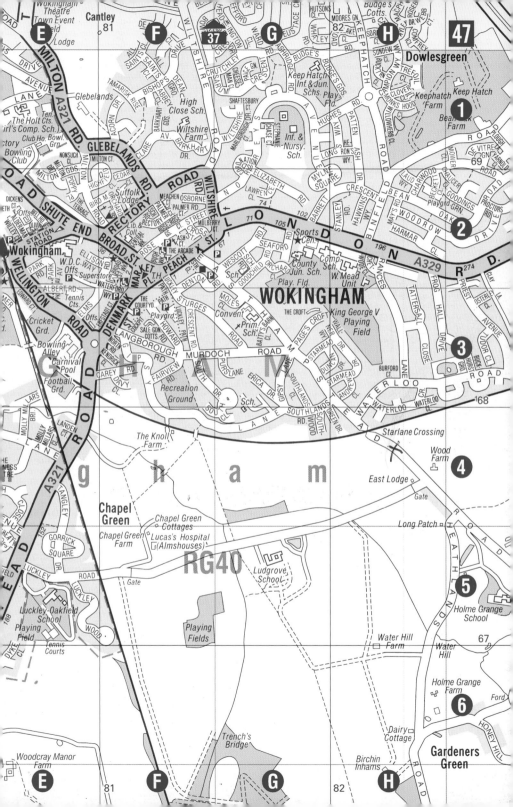

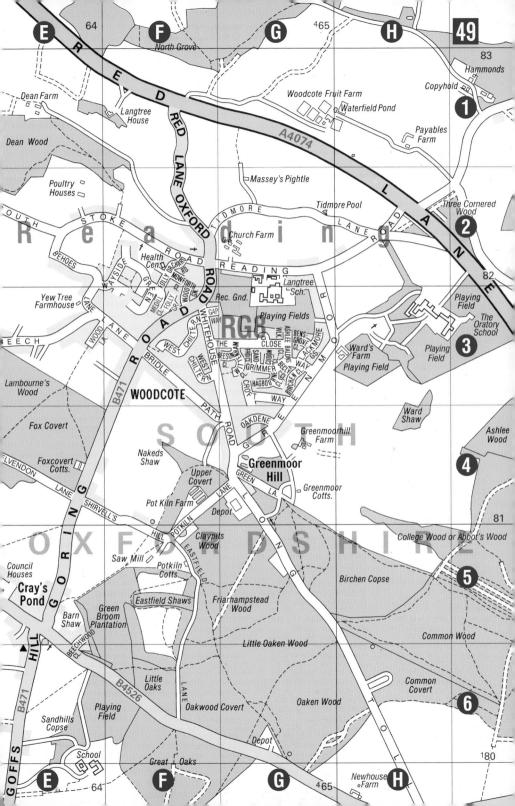

INDEX TO STREETS

HOW TO USE THIS INDEX

1. Each street name is followed by its Posttown or Postal Locality, and then by its map reference; e.g. Abattoirs Rd. Read —4B **22** is in the Reading Posttown and is to be found in square 4B on page **22**. The page number being shown in bold type.
A strict alphabetical order is followed in which Av., Rd., St., etc. (though abbreviated) are read in full and as part of the street name; e.g. Ashcroft Clo. appears after Ash Ct. but before Ashford Av.

2. Streets and a selection of Subsidiary names not shown on the Maps, appear in the index in *Italics* with the thoroughfare to which it is connected shown in brackets; e.g. *Abbotsbury Ho. Read —6D 32 (off Lulworth Rd.)*

3. With the now general usage of Postcodes for addressing mail, it is not recommended that this index is used for such a purpose.

GENERAL ABBREVIATIONS

All: Alley
App: Approach
Arc: Arcade
Av: Avenue
Bk: Back
Boulevd: Boulevard
Bri: Bridge
B'way: Broadway
Bldgs: Buildings
Bus: Business
Cen: Centre
Chu: Church
Chyd: Churchyard
Circ: Circle
Cir: Circus

Clo: Close
Comn: Common
Cotts: Cottages
Ct: Court
Cres: Crescent
Dri: Drive
E: East
Embkmt: Embankment
Est: Estate
Gdns: Gardens
Ga: Gate
Gt: Great
Grn: Green
Gro: Grove
Ho: House

Ind: Industrial
Junct: Junction
La: Lane
Lit: Little
Lwr: Lower
Mnr: Manor
Mans: Mansions
Mkt: Market
M: Mews
Mt: Mount
N: North
Pal: Palace
Pde: Parade
Pk: Park
Pas: Passage

Pl: Place
Rd: Road
S: South
Sq: Square
Sta: Station
St: Street
Ter: Terrace
Up: Upper
Vs: Villas
Wlk: Walk
W: West
Yd: Yard

POSTTOWN AND POSTAL LOCALITY ABBREVIATIONS

Arbor : Arborfield
Arbor X : Arborfield Cross
B'ham : Barkham
Binf : Binfield
Bin H : Binfield Heath
Bfld : Burghfield
Bfld C : Burghfield Common
Calc : Calcot
Cav : Caversham
Chalk : Chalkhouse Green
Charv : Charvil
Chaz H : Chazey Heath
C Grn : Cockpole Green
Cray P : Crays Pond
D'den : Dunsden
Ear : Earley
E Ils : East Ilsley
Emm G : Emmer Green

Eng : Englefield
Gall C : Gallowstree Common
Gor : Goring
Gor H : Goring Heath
Graz : Grazeley
Hare H : Hare Hatch
Harp : Harpsden
Hen T : Henley-on-Thames
Hurst : Hurst
Kid E : Kidmore End
Kiln G : Kiln Green
Know H : Knowl Hill
Land E : Lands End
Lwr Ear : Lower Earley
Lwr S : Lower Shiplake
Map : Mapledurham
Pang : Pangbourne
Pep C : Peppard Common

Ping : Pingewood
Play : Playhatch
Pur T : Purley on Thames
Read : Reading
Rem : Remenham
Roth P : Rothfield Peppard
Rusc : Ruscombe
Shin : Shinfield
S'lake : Shiplake
S'lake X : Shiplake Cross
Shur R : Shurlock Row
Sind : Sindlesham
Son : Sonning
Son C : Sonning Common
S Sto : South Stoke
Spen W : Spencers Wood
Streat : Streatley
Sul : Sulham

Sul'd : Sulhamstead
Thea : Theale
Three M : Three Mile Cross
Tid : Tidmarsh
Tile : Tilehurst
Tok G : Tokers Green
Twy : Twyford
Uff N : Ufton Nervet
Up Cul : Upper Culham
Wal L : Waltham St Lawrence
Warg : Wargrave
Whis G : Whistley Green
Whit T : Whitchurch on Thames
Winn : Winnersh
Wokgm : Wokingham
Woodc : Woodcote
Wdly : Woodley
Woos : Woosehill

INDEX TO STREETS

Abattoirs Rd. Read —4B **22**
Abbey Clo. Wokgm —1F **47**
Abbey Pk. Bfld C —5E **39**
Abbey Sq. Read —5C **22**
Abbey St. Read —4C **22**
Abbotsbury Ho. Read —6D 32
 (off Lulworth Rd.)
Abbots Ho. Read —4C 22
 (off Abbey St.)
Abbot's Rd. Bfld C —6E **39**
Abbots Wlk. Read —4C **22**
Aberaman. Cav —4A **12**
Aberford Clo. Read —5F **21**
Abingdon Dri. Cav —4D **12**
Abrahams Rd. Hen T —2B **2**
Acacia Rd. Read —6D **22**
Acorn Dri. Wokgm —1F **47**
Acorn Wlk. Calc —1H **29**
Acre Bus. Pk. Read —6C **32**
Acre Rd. Read —6B **32**
Adam Ct. Hen T —3D **2**
Adams Way. Ear —4G **33**
Addington Rd. Read —6E **23**
Addiscombe Chase. Tile —1G **19**
Addison Rd. Read —3B **22**

Adelaide Rd. Read —1H **33**
Adkins Rd. Wal L —3H **17**
Admiral's Ct. Read —1B **32**
Adwell Dri. Lwr Ear —5B **34**
Adwell Sq. Hen T —3C **2**
Agate Clo. Wokgm —1B **46**
Aggisters La. Wokgm —5H **45**
Agincourt Clo. Wokgm —2B **46**
Ainsdale Cres. Read —2D **30**
Alandale Clo. Read —6E **33**
Alan Pl. Read —1D **30**
Albany Pk. Dri. Winn —3F **35**
Albany Rd. Read —5G **21**
Albert Clo. Cav —6H **11**
Albert Rd. Hen T —4D **2**
Albert Rd. Wokgm —2E **47**
Albion Ter. Read —6D **22**
Albury Clo. Read —3F **21**
Albury Gdns. Calc —3B **30**
Aldbourne Av. Ear —2H **33**
Aldeburgh Clo. Read —4D **12**
Aldenham Clo. Cav —4D **12**
Alder Dri. Bfld C —5E **39**
Alder Dri. Tile —6H **19**
Alderfield Clo. Thea —2E **29**

Alderley Clo. Wdly —3E **25**
Alderman Willey Clo. Wokgm
 —2E **47**
Aldworth Clo. Read —1F **31**
Alexander Ct. Read —5A **22**
Alexandra Rd. Read —5E **23**
Alford Clo. Tile —4A **20**
Alfred St. Read —5A **22**
Alison Clo. Bfld C —6E **39**
Alison Wlk. Cav —2E **23**
Allcroft Rd. Read —1D **32**
Allendale Rd. Ear —3A **34**
All Hallows Rd. Cav —1E **23**
Allison Ct. Read —5A **22**
Allison Gdns. Pur T —5H **9**
Allnatt Av. Winn —5H **35**
Allonby Clo. Lwr Ear —4C **34**
All Saints Clo. Wokgm —1F **47**
Alma St. Read —4F **21**
Almond Clo. Wokgm —4H **45**
Almond Dri. Cav —6G **13**
Almshouses. Read —5B 22
 (off Castle St.)
Alpine St. Read —6C **22**
Alston Wlk. Cav —2E **23**

Amberley Dri. Twy —4A **16**
Amblecote Rd. Tile —5E **21**
Ambleside Clo. Wdly —5D **24**
Ambrook Rd. Read —6C **32**
Ambrose Pl. Read —5A **22**
Amersham Clo. Calc —2H **29**
Amersham Rd. Cav —2E **23**
Amethyst Clo. Wokgm —1A **46**
Amethyst La. Read —6F **21**
Amherst Rd. Read —6H **23**
Amity Rd. Read —5F **23**
Amity St. Read —4F **23**
Ammanford. Cav —5A **12**
Ancastle Grn. Hen T —4B **2**
Anderson Av. Ear —6H **23**
Anderson Cres. Arbor X —6D **44**
Andover Clo. Tile —3A **20**
Andrew Clo. Wokgm —3H **47**
Andrew's Clo. Thea —3D **28**
Andrews Rd. Ear —3A **34**
Angle Field Rd. Cav —1D **22**
Anglers Way. Read —5E **23**
Angus Clo. Calc —2B **30**
Annesley Gdns. Winn —4H **35**
Anson Cres. Read —1E **43**

Boathouse Reach. Hen T —4D **2**
Bobgreen Ct. Read —2D **42**
Bodmin Rd. Wdly —1B **34**
Body Rd. Read —5B **22**
Bolderwood. Bfld C —5E **39**
Bolney Rd. Lwr S —3C **6**
Bolney Trevor Dri. Lwr S —4B **6**
Bolwell Clo. Twy —6C **16**
Borrowdale Rd. Winn —2G **35**
Bosham Clo. Ear —6A **34**
Bostock La. Thea —4A **28**
Boston Av. Read —1A **32**
Boston Rd. Hen T —5D **2**
Bosworth Gdns. Wdly —2D **34**
Bothy, The. Warg —6E **7**
Bottisham Clo. Lwr Ear —6B **34**
Bottom Ho. Son C —4E **5**
Bottom La. Sul'd —1B **38**
Boulters Clo. Wdly —4E **25**
Boulton Rd. Read —3B **32**
Boult St. Read —5D **22**
Boult's Wlk. Read —1C **32**
Boundary Clo. Tile —6H **19**
Boundary La. Cav —1H **21**
Bourn Clo. Lwr Ear —5B **34**
Bourne Av. Read —2C **32**
Bourne Clo. Calc —2G **29**
Bourne Rd. Pang —5C **8**
Bourton Clo. Tile —5C **20**
Bower Cres. Wokgm —6F **37**
Bowfell Clo. Tile —2H **19**
Bowling Ct. Hen T —2C **2**
Bowling Grn. La. Pur T —5G **9**
Bowyer Cres. Wokgm —6F **37**
Bracken Clo. Tile —3H **19**
Brackendale Way. Read —1H **33**
Bracken Way. Bfld C —6F **39**
Brading Way. Pur T —5A **10**
Bradmore Way. Lwr Ear —6H **33**
Bradwell Rd. Tile —1H **19**
Bramber M. Cav —6F **13**
Bramble Cres. Tile —4B **20**
Bramblings. Cav —4H **11**
Bramley Clo. Ear —3F **21**
Bramley Cres. Son C —3D **4**
Brampton Chase. Lwr S —4B **6**
Bramshaw Rd. Read —3D **20**
Bran Clo. Tile —4B **20**
Brandon Av. Wdly —3F **25**
Branksome Ct. Read —5A **22**
Brant Clo. Arbor X —6D **44**
Braybrook Dri. Hurst —4C **26**
Braybrooke Gdns. Warg —1A **16**
Brayford Rd. Read —6D **32**
Bray Rd. Read —2E **31**
Brean Wlk. Ear —4H **33**
Brechin Ct. Read —6D 22
(off Kendrick Rd.)
Brecon Rd. Wdly —4E **25**
Bredon Rd. Wokgm —5C **36**
Breedon's Hill. Pang —5B **8**
Brendon Clo. Tile —3B **20**
Brent Gdns. Read —3C **32**
Brerewood. Ear —4G **33**
Briant's Av. Cav —2D **22**
Briar Clo. Cav —5B **12**
Briars Clo. Pang —5D **8**
Bridge Ho. Read —4C **22**
Bridges Clo. Wokgm —1C **46**
Bridges Hall. Read —1G **33**
Bridge St. Cav —2B **22**
Bridge St. Read —5B **22**
Bridge St. Plaza. Read —5B **22**
Bridgewater Clo. Read —3F **21**
Bridle Path. Woodc —3F **49**
Brierly Pl. Tile —6H **9**
Brigham Rd. Read —3B **22**

Brighton Pl. Read —6H **23**
Brighton Rd. Read —6H **23**
Brill Clo. Cav —6B **12**
Brimblecombe Clo. Wokgm
—5D **36**
Brimpton Rd. Read —2E **31**
Brinds Clo. Son C —3F **5**
Briony Rd. Read —1C **42**
Brisbane Rd. Read —4E **21**
Bristow Ct. Cav —2C **22**
Britten Rd. Read —2C **32**
Brixham Rd. Read —4C **32**
Broadcommon Rd. Hurst —4D **26**
Broad Hinton. Twy —1C **26**
Broadlands Clo. Calc —1A **30**
Broadmoor La. Son —6D **14**
Broad St. Read —5B **22**
Broad St. Wokgm —2F **47**
Broad St. Mall, The. Read —5B **22**
Broad St. Wlk. Wokgm —2F **47**
Broadwater La. Twy —2B **26**
Broadwater Rd. Twy —1B **26**
Brock Gdns. Read —4F **21**
Brockley Clo. Tile —4D **20**
Brocks Way. S'lake —5B **6**
Bromley Wlk. Tile —5C **20**
Brompton Clo. Lwr Ear —5C **34**
Brook Clo. Wokgm —6D **36**
Brooker's Hill. Shin —2E **43**
Brook La. Wal L —2H **27**
Brook Lea. Cav —3D **22**
Brooklyn Dri. Emm G —3C **12**
Brookmill, The. Read —2H **31**
Brooksby Rd. Tile —2A **20**
Brookside. Calc —2C 30
(off Millers Gro.)
Brookside. Wokgm —1C **46**
Brookside Clo. Ear —3C **34**
Brook St. Twy —6A **16**
Brook St. W. Read —6B **22**
Broom Clo. Calc —1H **29**
Broomfield Rd. Tile —4C **20**
Broom Gro. Wokgm —4A **46**
Broughton Clo. Read —3F **21**
Brownlow Rd. Read —5H **21**
Bruce Rd. Wdly —5C **24**
Brunel Arc. Read —4C **22**
Brunel Dri. Wdly —3E **25**
Brunel Rd. Read —2D **30**
Brunel Rd. Thea —4D **28**
Brunswick Hill. Read —5H **21**
Brunswick Lodge. Read —5H 21
(off Brunswick Hill)
Brunswick St. Read —5H **21**
Brybur Clo. Read —5E **33**
Buccaneer Clo. Wdly —4G **25**
Buckden Clo. Wdly —6F **25**
Buckhurst Gro. Wokgm —3H **47**
Buckhurst Way. Ear —3H **33**
Buckingham Dri. Emm G —6C **12**
(in three parts)
Buckland Rd. Read —3C **32**
Bucknell Av. Pang —5D **8**
Bucknell Clo. Read —2C· **30**
Buckside. Cav —2B **22**
Buckthorn Clo. Wokgm —1H **47**
Budge's Gdns. Wokgm —1G **47**
Budge's Rd. Wokgm —1G **47**
Bull Meadow, The. Streat —5A **48**
Bulmershe Rd. Read —5F **23**
Bunces La. Bfld C —6F **39**
Bungalow Dri. Tile —4A **20**
Burbidge Clo. Calc —3C **30**
Burcombe Way. Emm G —6C **12**
Burdett Ct. Read —3D **22**
Burdock Clo. Bfld C —6G **39**
Burford Ct. Read —4A **22**
Burford Ct. Wokgm —3H **47**
Burgess Clo. Wdly —2C **34**

Burghfield Rd. Read —5C **30**
Burleigh M. Cav —4D **12**
Burlingham Clo. Read —2D **42**
Burlington Rd. Tile —5A **20**
Burnham Rise. Emm G —3D **12**
Burnistone Clo. Lwr Ear —4D **34**
Burns Clo. Wdly —2D **34**
Burnthouse La. Ping —3E **41**
Burrcroft Ct. Read —1D **30**
Burrcroft Rd. Read —1D **30**
Burwell Clo. Lwr Ear —5B **34**
Bush Wlk. Wokgm —2F **47**
Business Cen., The. Wokgm
—4E **47**
Bute St. Read —1E **31**
Butler's Orchard. Kid E —5C **4**
Butter Mkt. Read —5C **22**
Butts Cen. Read —5B 22
(off Castle St.)
Butts Hill Rd. Son & Wdly —2D **24**
Buxton Av. Cav —6A **12**
Byefield Rd. Read —2E **31**
Byreton Clo. Ear —4A **34**
Byron Clo. Twy —6B **16**
Byron Rd. Ear —5H **23**
Byron Rd. Twy —6B **16**
Bythorn Clo. Lwr Ear —4D **34**
Byworth Clo. Read —1C **42**

Cadogan Clo. Cav —6E **13**
Cadogan Clo. Tile —5B **20**
Caistor Clo. Calc —2G **29**
Calbourne Dri. Calc —2A **30**
Calcot Pl. Dri. Calc —2B **30**
Caldbeck Dri. Wdly —5D **24**
Calder Clo. Tile —4C **20**
Caleta Clo. Ear —2E **23**
Callington Rd. Read —5C **32**
Calshot Pl. Calc —2A **30**
Cambourne Clo. Lwr Ear —5H **33**
Cambrian Way. Calc —2A **30**
Cambridgeshire Clo. Wokgm
—2B **46**
Cambridge St. Read —4H **21**
Camden Pl. Calc —2G **29**
Camellia Way. Wokgm —1A **46**
Campbell Rd. Wdly —1C **34**
Campion Way. Wokgm —6H **37**
Camp Rd. Uft N —5B **38**
Canal Way. Read —5E **23**
Canford Ct. Read —5G **21**
Cannock Way. Lwr Ear —5B **34**
Cannon St. Read —4H **21**
Canterbury Rd. Read —3C **32**
Cantley Cres. Wokgm —6D **36**
Caraway Rd. Ear —5H **33**
Cardiff M. Read —3A **22**
Cardiff Rd. Read —3H **21**
Cardigan Gdns. Read —1F **33**
Cardigan Rd. Read —6F **23**
Cardinal Clo. Cav —2C **22**
Carew Clo. Tile —6G **9**
Carey Rd. Wokgm —3F **47**
Carey St. Read —5A **22**
Cariad Ct. Gor —4B **48**
Carisbrooke Clo. Cav —4D **12**
Carland Clo. Lwr Ear —5H **33**
Carlile Gdns. Twy —3A **16**
Carling Rd. Son C —2D **4**
Carlisle Rd. Tile —2B **20**
(in two parts)
Carlton Clo. Wdly —6D **24**
Carlton Rd. Cav —5G **11**
Carnarvon Rd. Read —5F **23**
Carnoustie Ct. Read —5E 23
(off Muirfield Clo.)
Caroline Ct. Read —6H **21**
Caroline Dri. Wokgm —1D **46**

Caroline St. Read —4A **22**
Carrick Gdns. Wdly —5B **24**
Carron Clo. Tile —5D **20**
Carsdale Clo. Read —1A **32**
Carshalton Way. Lwr Ear —5B **34**
Carston Gro. Calc —2C **30**
Carter's Hill. Wokgm & Brack
—2H **37**
Cartershill La. Arbor —4C **44**
Carters Rise. Calc —2B **30**
Cartmel Dri. Wdly —6C **24**
Cassia Dri. Ear —5G **33**
Castle Cres. Read —6A **22**
Castle End Rd. Rusc —4C **16**
Castle Hill. Read —6A **22**
Castle St. Read —5B **22**
Catalina Clo. Wdly —5G **25**
Catcliffe Way. Lwr Ear —6G **33**
Catherine St. Read —4G **21**
Causmans Way. Tile —3H **19**
Cavalier Clo. Thea —2C **28**
Cavendish Gdns. Winn —3F **35**
Cavendish Rd. Cav —4D **12**
Caversham Pk. Dri. Cav —5D **12**
Caversham Pk. Rd. Cav —4D **12**
Caversham Rd. Read —4B **22**
Caversham Wharf. Read —3B **22**
Cawsam Gdns. Cav —6D **12**
Caxton Clo. Read —3F **21**
Caxton Ct. Hen T —4D **2**
Cecil Aldin Dri. Tile —5H **9**
Cedar Clo. Wokgm —2F **47**
Cedar Dri. Pang —6B **8**
Cedar Lodge. Hen T —5E **3**
Cedar Rd. Read —5F **33**
Cedars, The. Tile —2A **20**
Cedar Wood Cres. Cav —6C **12**
Central Wlk. Wokgm —2F **47**
Centurion Clo. Read —6B **22**
Chaffinch Clo. Tile —5G **19**
Chaffinch Clo. Wokgm —3B **46**
Chagford Rd. Read —5C **32**
Chain St. Read —5B **22**
Chalcraft Clo. Hen T —5B **2**
Chalfont Clo. Ear —5H **33**
Chalfont Way. Ear —5H **33**
Chalgrove Way. Emm G —4D **12**
Chalkhouse Grn. La. Chalk —1B **12**
(in two parts)
Chalkhouse Grn. Rd. Kid E —5C **4**
Chamberlains Gdns. Arbor X
—6D **44**
Chambers, The. Read —5C 22
(off East St.)
Champion Rd. Cav —3D **22**
Chancellor's Way, The. Ear —2F **33**
Chancery M. Read —5A **22**
Chapel Hill. Tile —4H **19**
Chapel La. Spen W —6C **42**
Chapel Row. Twy —6A **16**
Chard Clo. Wdly —6D **24**
Charfield Ct. Read —5F **23**
Charles Clore Ct. Read —2D **30**
Charles Evans Way. Cav —2E **23**
Charles St. Read —4A **22**
Charndon Clo. Read —1C **32**
Charrington Rd. Calc —2G **29**
Charvil Ho. Rd. Charv —5F **15**
Charvil La. Son —1D **24**
Charville Dri. Calc —2G **29**
Charwood Rd. Wokgm —2H **47**
Chaseside Av. Twy —3A **16**
Chase, The. Calc —2A **30**
Chatham St. Read —4A **22**
Chatsworth Av. Winn —4F **35**
Chatsworth Clo. Cav —4D **12**
Chatteris Way. Lwr Ear —5A **34**
Chatton Clo. Lwr Ear —6H **33**
Chaucer Clo. Emm G —5B **12**

Chaucer Clo. Wokgm —2H **47**
Chaucer Way. Wokgm —3B **46**
Chazey Clo. Chaz H —2F **11**
Chazey Rd. Cav —6G **11**
Cheapside. Read —4B **22**
Cheddington Clo. Tile —6C **20**
Cheeseman Clo. Wokgm —1G **47**
Chelford Way. Cav —6A **12**
Chelsea Clo. Tile —3C **20**
Chelwood Rd. Ear —4A **34**
Chepstow Rd. Tile —2A **20**
Chequers Way. Wdly —5B **24**
Cheriton Av. Twy —4A **16**
Cheriton Ct. Read —6B **22**
Cheriton Pl. Son C —4E **5**
Cherry Clo. Cav —2D **12**
Cherrytree Gro. Wokgm —4H **45**
Chervil Way. Bfld C —6G **39**
Cherwell Cres. Read —5A 22
  (off Trinity Pl.)
Cherwell Rd. Cav —4B **12**
Chesterman St. Read —6C **22**
Chester St. Cav —2B **22**
Chester St. Read —4G **21**
Chestnut Av. Cav —6F **13**
Chestnut Av. Wokgm —2H **45**
Chestnut Clo. Thea —2D **28**
Chestnut Cotts. Streat —5A **48**
Chestnut Cres. Shin —4F **43**
Chestnut Dri. Bfld —4G **39**
Chestnut Gro. Pur T —5A **10**
Chestnuts, The. S'lake —5B **6**
Chestnut Wlk. Read —5C **22**
Chetwode Clo. Wokgm —2H **47**
Cheviot Dri. Charv —6G **15**
Chichester Rd. Tile —4B **20**
Chicory Clo. Ear —5G **33**
Chievley Clo. Tile —4H **19**
Chilcombe Way. Lwr Ear —4C **34**
Childrey Way. Tile —4G **19**
Childs Hall. Read —1G **33**
Chiltern Bank. Pep C —1C **4**
Chiltern Clo. Hen T —5A **2**
Chiltern Ct. Emm G —4B **12**
Chiltern Cres. Ear —5H **23**
Chiltern Dri. Charv —6G **15**
Chiltern Rd. Cav —6D **12**
Chiltern Rd. Pep C —1C **4**
Chiltern View. Pur T —5A **10**
Chiltern Wlk. Pang —5C **8**
Chippenham Clo. Lwr Ear —6G **33**
Chittering Clo. Lwr Ear —5B **34**
Chive Rd. Ear —5H **33**
Cholmeley Pl. Read —5F **23**
Cholmeley Rd. Read —4F **23**
Cholmeley Ter. Read —5F **23**
Christchurch Ct. Read —1D **32**
Christchurch Gdns. Read —1D **32**
Christchurch Rd. Read —1D **32**
Chudleigh Gdns. Read —4D **32**
Church Av. Hen T —1D **2**
Church Clo. Winn —4H **35**
Church Cotts. Read —6B **20**
Church End La. Tile —5C **20**
Church Hill. Hurst —6B **26**
Churchill Clo. Read —4C **32**
Churchill Cres. Son C —2E **5**
Churchill Dri. Winn —4G **35**
Church La. Arbor —4B **44**
Church La. B'ham —6H **45**
Church La. Roth P —1F **5**
Church La. Rusc —5C **16**
Church La. S'lake —1E **15**
Church La. Three M & Shin
  —4C **42**
Church La. Uft N —3A **38**
Church M. Pur T —5A **10**
Church M. Wdly —4E **25**
Church Rd. Cav —2A **22**

Church Rd. Ear —1A **34**
Church Rd. Pang —5B **8**
Church Rd. Wdly —4E **25**
Church St. Cav —2B **22**
Church St. Hen T —4C **2**
Church St. Read —6C **22**
Church St. Thea —3C **28**
Church St. Twy —6A **16**
Church St. Warg —6D **5**
Church Ter. Read —6B 22
  (off Dover St.)
Churchward Wlk. Calc —2C **30**
Cinnamon Clo. Ear —5G **33**
Cintra Av. Read —2D **32**
Circuit La. Read —1E **31**
City Rd. Tile —6G **19**
Clanfield Cres. Tile —2H **19**
Clare Av. Wokgm —1F **47**
Clarence Rd. Hen T —3C **2**
Clarence Way. Calc —2G **29**
Clarendon Clo. Winn —4A **36**
Clarendon Rd. Read —6H **23**
Clares Grn. Spen W —5C **42**
Clay Clo. Tile —3G **19**
Claydon Ct. Cav —3B **22**
Clayhill Rd. Bfld C & Bfld —5E **39**
Clay La. Wokgm —2H **47**
Clayton Wlk. Read —2D **32**
Cleeve Ct. Streat —4B **48**
Cleeve Down. Gor —4D **48**
Cleeve Rd. Gor —4B **48**
Clements Mead. Tile —4G **19**
Clements Rd. Hen T —2B **2**
Clent Rd. Read —2C **32**
Clevedon Dri. Ear —4H **33**
Clevedon Rd. Tile —1B **20**
Cleveland. Charv —6G **15**
Clevemede. Gor —4C **48**
Clifton Pk. Rd. Cav —1A **22**
Clifton Rise. Warg —1B **16**
Clifton Rd. Wokgm —6D **36**
Clifton St. Read —5A **22**
Clivedale Rd. Wdly —2D **34**
Cloister M. Thea —3D **28**
Cloisters, The. Cav —1B **22**
Close, The. Bfld C —5F **39**
Close, The. Hen T —5C **2**
Close, The. Woodc —3G **49**
Close, The. Wdly —1D **34**
Clove Clo. Lwr Ear —5G **33**
Clover Clo. Wokgm —1H **47**
Coach Horse Ct. Pang —5D **8**
Coalport Way. Tile —3B **20**
Cobham Rd. Wdly —5E **25**
Cockney Hill. Tile —6C **20**
Cockpit Path. Wokgm —3F **47**
Cody Clo. Wdly —4G **25**
Coldharbour Clo. Hen T —5B **2**
Coldicutt St. Cav —3D **22**
Cole La. Arbor X —5D **44**
Colemans Moor La. Wdly —6E **25**
Colemans Moor Rd. Wdly —2E **35**
Coleridge Clo. Twy —1C **26**
Coley Av. Read —1A **32**
  (in two parts)
Coley Hill. Read —6A **22**
Coley Pk. Rd. Read —6A **22**
Coley Pl. Read —6B **22**
College Rd. Read —6G **23**
Colleton Dri. Twy —6B **16**
Colliers Way. Read —5E **21**
Collingwood Wlk. Read —5G **19**
Collis St. Read —1C **32**
Colliston Wlk. Calc —3C **30**
Colmworth Clo. Lwr Ear —6H **33**
Colston Clo. Calc —2A **30**
Coltsfoot Clo. Bfld C —5G **39**
Colyton Way. Pur T —5H **9**
Combe Rd. Tile —5C **20**

Comet Way. Wdly —5F **25**
Comfrey Clo. Wokgm —6H **37**
Commercial Rd. Read —5B **32**
Common Hill. Eng —3A **28**
Commons Rd. Wokgm —5C **36**
Compton Av. Tile —5G **19**
Compton Clo. Ear —2B **34**
Concorde Way. Wdly —5F **25**
Condor Clo. Tile —1H **19**
Conifer Dri. Tile —2G **19**
Coningham Rd. Read —2D **42**
Conisboro Av. Cav —5H **11**
Conisboro Way. Cav —5H **11**
Coniston Clo. Wdly —1E **35**
Coniston Dri. Tile —2C **20**
Connaught Clo. Read —5G **21**
Connaught Rd. Read —5G **21**
Constitution Rd. Read —4E **21**
Consul Clo. Wdly —1E **35**
Conway Rd. Calc —1H **29**
Conygree Clo. Lwr Ear —5A **34**
Coombes La. Wokgm —4F **45**
Coombe, The. .Streat —5A **48**
Cooper Clo. Read —1D **42**
Cooper Rd. Hen T —2C **2**
Coopers Pightle. Kid E —5C **4**
Copenhagen Clo. Read —1D **42**
Copperdale Clo. Ear —3G **33**
Coppice Rd. Wdly —2D **34**
Copse Av. Cav —1E **23**
Copse Barnhill La. Wokgm
  —2E **45**
Copse Clo. Tile —1A **20**
Copse Dri. Wokgm —1D **46**
Copse Mead. Wdly —3E **25**
Copse, The. Warg —5F **7**
Corbett Gdns. Wdly —5D **24**
Corbridge Rd. Read —2D **32**
Corby Clo. Wdly —3F **25**
Corfe M. Cav —6F **13**
Coriander Way. Ear —5G **33**
Corinne Clo. Read —5C **32**
Cornfield Grn. Wokgm —6C **36**
Cornfield Rd. Wdly —4F **25**
Cornflower Clo. Wokgm —1A **46**
Cornwall Clo. Tile —6G **9**
Cornwall Clo. Wokgm —2A **46**
Cornwood Gdns. Read —3D **32**
Coronation Cotts. Hurst —2A **36**
Coronation Sq. Read —2E **31**
Coronation Sq. Wokgm —1G **47**
Corsham Rd. Calc —3C **30**
Corwen Rd. Tile —4A **20**
Cotswold Way. Tile —2G **19**
Cottage La. Ping —4F **31**
Cotterell Gdns. Twy —1C **26**
Cottesmore Rd. Wdly —6C **24**
Courtenay Dri. Emm G —3C **12**
Courtlands Hill. Pang —6B **8**
Courts Rd. Ear —2A **34**
Courtyard, The. Thea —3D **28**
Courtyard, The. Wokgm —3F **47**
Coventry Rd. Read —4F **23**
Cow La. E Ils —1A **48**
Cow La. Read —2H **21**
  (in two parts)
Cowper Way. Read —2G **31**
Cowslip Clo. Tile —6G **19**
Cradock Rd. Read —2B **32**
Craig Av. Read —4E **21**
Crail Clo. Wokgm —5D **46**
Cranborne Gdns. Read —2D **20**
Cranbourne Av. Calc —2H **29**
Cranbury Rd. Read —5G **21**
Crane Wharf. Read —5C **22**
Cranford Clo. Hurst —4C **26**
Cranmer Clo. Tile —1G **19**
Craven Rd. Read —6E **23**
Crawford Clo. Ear —3A **34**

Crawshay Dri. Emm G —3C **12**
Craysleaze. Kid E —5C **4**
Crecy Clo. Wokgm —2B **46**
Crediton Clo. Wdly —6F **25**
Creighton Ct. Read —2E **33**
Cremyll Rd. Read —3A **22**
Crendon Ct. Cav —2B **22**
Crescent Ho. Wdly —1D **34**
Crescent Rd. Read —6F **23**
Crescent Rd. Tile —3A **20**
Crescent Rd. Wokgm —3F **47**
Crescent, The. Ear —2B **34**
Crescent, The. S'lake —4C **6**
Crescent, The. Thea —2C **28**
Cressingham Rd. Read —3D **32**
Crest Clo. Rusc —4B **16**
Creswell Clo. Read —2D **42**
Crispin Clo. Cav —5G **11**
Crisp Rd. Hen T —2B **2**
Crockhamwell Rd. Wdly —6D **24**
Crocus Way. Wokgm —1A **46**
Croft Clo. Wokgm —6D **46**
Croft Rd. Gor —5C **48**
Croft Rd. Spen W —6D **42**
Croft Rd. Wokgm —6D **46**
Croft, The. Wokgm —3G **47**
Croft Way. Woodc —3G **49**
Cromer Clo. Tile —3H **19**
Cromwell Clo. Hen T —5C **2**
Cromwell Rd. Cav —2C **22**
Cromwell Rd. Hen T —5D **2**
Crosfields Clo. Read —6D **32**
Crossland Rd. Read —5C **22**
Cross St. Read —4C **22**
Cross St. Wokgm —2F **47**
Crossways. Wdly —1D **34**
Crown La. Thea —3D **28**
Crown Pl. Read —6D **22**
Crown St. Read —6C **22**
Crowsley Rd. S'lake —4B **6**
Crowsley Way. Son C —3D **4**
Crutchley Rd. Wokgm —1G **47**
Cuddesdon Clo. Woodc —3G **49**
Culford Clo. Lwr Ear —4C **34**
Culloden Way. Wokgm —2B **46**
Culver La. Ear —5H **23**
Culver Rd. Read —6G **23**
Cumberland Rd. Read —4E **23**
Cumberland Way. Wokgm —2A **46**
Curlew Dri. Tile —6H **19**
Curl Way. Wokgm —3D **46**
Curtis Rd. Calc —1H **29**
Curzon St. Read —4G **21**
Cusden Wlk. Read —5B 22
  (off Castle St.)
Cutbush Clo. Lwr Ear —6A **34**
Cutbush La. Lwr Ear —6H **33**
Cutbush La. Shin —2F **43**
Cwmcarn. Cav —4A **12**
Cypress Rd. Wdly —6F **25**

Dacre Av. Cav —6F **13**
Dale Rd. Read —1C **32**
Dalton Clo. Tile —4B **20**
Damer Gdns. Hen T —5D **2**
Danehill. Lwr Ear —6A **34**
Danywern Dri. Winn —4H **35**
Darell Rd. Cav —1A **22**
Dark La. Tile —2G **19**
Dartington Av. Wdly —2C **34**
Dartington Clo. Tile —4C **20**
Dartmouth Ter. Read —6C **22**
Darvills La. Read —3H **27**
Darwin Clo. Read —5B **32**
Dauntless Rd. Bfld C —4G **39**
David Smith Ct. Calc —1C **30**
Davis Clo. Winn —5G **35**
Davis St. Hurst —3H **35**

Davis Way. Hurst —2A **36**
Davy Clo. Wokgm —3F **47**
Dawlish Rd. Read —4D **32**
Deacon Clo. Wokgm —6F **37**
Deaconfield. S Sto —1C **48**
Deacon Way. Tile —2D **20**
Deadman's La. Thea —2C **28**
Deanfield Av. Hen T —4C **2**
Deanfield Rd. Hen T —4B **2**
Dean Gro. Wokgm —1F **47**
Deansgate Rd. Read —6C **22**
De Beauvoir Rd. Read —5F **23**
De Bohun Rd. Read —3C **22**
Deepdene Clo. Read —5H **21**
Deerhurst Av. Winn —4H **35**
Deerhurst Clo. Calc —2B **30**
Dee Rd. Tile —6C **20**
Defford Clo. Wokgm —5C **36**
Delafield Dri. Calc —2H **29**
Delamere Rd. Ear —4A **24**
Delane Dri. Winn —5G **35**
Delaney Clo. Tile —4C **20**
Delft Clo. Tile —4C **20**
Dell Rd. Tile —2H **19**
Dell, The. Read —5D **22**
Delph, The. Lwr Ear —4D **34**
De Montfort Rd. Read —3B **22**
Dempsey Ho. Read —5C **20**
Denbury Gdns. Read —6D **32**
Denby Way. Tile —3C **20**
Dene Clo. Ear —3H **33**
Denhose Clo. Lwr Ear —5H **33**
Denmark Av. Wdly —3F **25**
Denmark Rd. Read —5E **23**
Denmark St. Wokgm —3F **47**
Denton Rd. Wokgm —2F **47**
Derby Rd. Cav —1C **22**
Derby St. Read —4A **22**
Derrick Clo. Calc —2H **29**
Derwent Av. Tile —2B **20**
Derwent Clo. Wokgm —2B **46**
Deveron Dri. Read —5C **20**
Devil's Hill. Roth P —3H **5**
De Vitre Grn. Wokgm —1H **47**
Devitt Clo. Read —5G **33**
Devon Clo. Wokgm —2B **46**
Devon Dri. Cav —6F **13**
Devonshire Gdns. Tile —1G **19**
Devonshire Pk. Read —4F **33**
Diamond Way. Wokgm —1B **46**
Dickens Ct. Wokgm —2E **47**
Dieppe Clo. Wokgm —2B **46**
Doddington Clo. Lwr Ear —5B **34**
Doles Hill. B'ham —5A **46**
Doles La. Wokgm —4B **46**
Dolphin Clo. Winn —5H **35**
Donaldson Way. Wdly —4F **25**
Don Clo. Tile —4D **20**
Donegal Clo. Cav —1D **22**
Donkin Hill. Cav —1D **22**
Donnington Gdns. Read —6E **23**
Donnington Pl. Winn —4A **36**
Donnington Rd. Read —5E **23**
Dorchester Ct. Read —6F **21**
Dorking Way. Calc —2F **29**
Dorothy St. Read —6C **22**
Dorset St. Read —4F **21**
Dorset Way. Wokgm —2B **46**
Douglas Ct. Ear —3H **33**
Douglas Grange. Hurst —2A **36**
Douglas Rd. Cav —2E **23**
Dove Clo. Lwr Ear —6G **33**
Dovecote Rd. Read —1C **42**
Dovedale Clo. Cav —1A **22**
Dover St. Read —6B **22**
Dowding Way. Wdly —5F **25**
Downham Ct. Read —5F **33**
Downing Rd. Tile —4A **20**
Downshire Sq. Read —6H **21**

Downs Way. Tile —2H **19**
Drawback Hill. Hen T —6C **2**
Dray's La. Roth P —1F **5**
Drayton Rd. Read —4E **21**
Dresden Way. Tile —3C **20**
Drewett Clo. Read —2D **42**
Drive, The. Ear —5H **23**
Drome Path. Winn —3F **35**
Drovers Way. Wdly —1D **34**
Dryland Ho. Read —5C **20**
Duchess Clo. Whit T —3C **8**
Dudley Clo. Tile —3B **20**
Dudley M. Tile —2B **20**
Duffield Rd. Son & Wdly —2D **24**
Dukesbridge Ct. Read —5C 22
(off Duke St.)
Duke St. Hen T —3D **2**
Duke St. Read —5C **22**
Dulnan Clo. Tile —4D **20**
Dulverton Gdns. Read —4D **32**
Dumbarton Way. Cav —5F **13**
Dunaways Clo. Ear —3C **34**
Dunbar Dri. Wdly —6F **25**
Duncan Dri. Wokgm —3G **47**
Duncan Gdns. Pur T —6H **9**
Duncan Rd. Wdly —6D **24**
Dundela Clo. Wdly —6D **24**
Dunholme Clo. Lwr Ear —4D **34**
Dunkirk Clo. Wokgm —2B **46**
Dunluce Gdns. Pang —5D **8**
Dunnock Way. Warg —5F **7**
Dunoon Clo. Calc —2B **30**
Dunsden Way. Bin H —1H **13**
Dunsfold Rd. Tile —5C **20**
Dunstall Clo. Tile —4A **20**
Dunster Clo. Cav —4D **12**
Dunt Av. Hurst —2B **36**
Dunt La. Hurst —1A **36**
Durand Rd. Ear —5H **33**
Durham Clo. Read —6D **32**
Durham Clo. Wokgm —2B **46**
Dusseldorf Way. Read —5B **22**
Dwyer Rd. Read —2C **30**
Dysonswood La. Tok G —2H **11**

Earley Hill Rd. Read —1H **33**
Earley Pl. Read —5C **22**
Earlsfield Clo. Cav —6F **13**
Easington Dri. Lwr Ear —4D **34**
Eastbury Av. Tile —4G **19**
Eastbury Pk. Winn —4A **36**
Eastcourt Av. Ear —6H **23**
East Dri. Calc —1B **30**
Eastern Av. Read —5F **23**
Eastern Ct. Read —6F **23**
Eastfield La. Gor H —6F **49**
Eastfield La. Whit T —3C **8**
Easthampstead Rd. Wokgm
—2G **47**
Eastheath Av. Wokgm —4E **47**
Eastheath Gdns. Wokgm —5E **47**
East La. Rusc —4D **16**
East St. Read —5C **22**
E. View Clo. Warg —6F **7**
E. View Rd. Warg —6F **7**
Eastwood Ct. Wdly —2D **34**
Eastwood Rd. Wdly —2D **34**
Eaton Ct. Read —5A 22
(off Oxford Rd.)
Eaton Pl. Read —5A **22**
Ebborne Sq. Lwr Ear —5B **34**
Eccles Clo. Cav —2D **22**
Edenhall Clo. Tile —4D **20**
Edenham Clo. Lwr Ear —5D **34**
Edenham Cres. Read —1H **31**
Eden Way. Winn —5G **35**
Edgar Milward Clo. Tile —3D **20**

Edgehill St. Read —1C **32**
Edinburgh Rd. Read —5H **21**
Edneys Hill. Wokgm —5A **46**
Edward Ct. Wokgm —3E **47**
Edward Rd. Charv —5G **15**
Egerton Rd. Read —5F **33**
Egremont Dri. Lwr Ear —3C **34**
Elan Clo. Tile —5C **20**
Eldart Clo. Tile —5E **21**
Elder Clo. Tile —3H **19**
Eldon Pl. Read —5D **22**
Eldon Rd. Read —5D **22**
Eldon Sq. Read —5E **23**
Eldon St. Read —5E **23**
Eldon Ter. Read —5E **23**
Elford Clo. Lwr Ear —5B **34**
Elgar Rd. Read —6B **22**
Elgar Rd. S. Read —1C **32**
Eliot Clo. Cav —6B **12**
Elizabeth Clo. Hen T —5A **2**
Elizabeth Ct. Thea —3D **28**
Elizabeth Ct. Tile —3A **20**
Elizabeth Ct. Warg —6E **7**
Elizabeth Ct. Wokgm —2E **47**
Elizabeth M. Read —5C **22**
Elizabeth Rd. Hen T —5A **2**
Elizabeth Rd. Wokgm —2G **47**
Elizabeth Rout Clo. Spen W
—6D **42**
Elizabeth Wlk. Read —1C **32**
Ellerton Clo. Thea —2D **28**
Ellesmere Clo. Cav —1C **22**
Ellison Way. Wokgm —2E **47**
Ellis's Hill. Arbor —4E **45**
Elm Ct. Son C —4F **5**
Elmcroft. Gor —6C **48**
Elm Dri. Bfld —3G **39**
Elmhurst Rd. Gor —4C **48**
Elmhurst Rd. Read —1E **33**
Elm La. Lwr Ear —4G **33**
(in two parts)
Emleigh Ct. Cav —1D **22**
Elmley Clo. Wokgm —5C **36**
Elm Lodge Av. Read —4G **21**
Elm Pk. Read —5G **21**
Elm Pk. Rd. Read —5G **21**
Elm Rd. Lwr Ear —4F **33**
Elm Rd. Tok G —3G **11**
Elms Rd. Wokgm —3E **47**
Elmstone Dri. Tile —3H **19**
Elsley Rd. Tile —1A **20**
Elstow Av. Cav —4D **12**
Elstree Clo. Tile —2A **20**
Eltham Av. Cav —5F **13**
Elvaston Way. Tile —5C **20**
Elveden Clo. Lwr Ear —4D **34**
Elvendon Rd. Gor —4C **48**
Elyham. Pur T —5G **9**
Ely Rd. Thea —4D **28**
Emblen Cres. Arbor X —6D **44**
Embrook Way. Calc —2F **29**
Emerald Clo. Wokgm —1B **46**
Emma La. Warg —6F **7**
Emmbrook Ct. Read —4F **33**
Emmbrook Ga. Wokgm —6C **36**
Emmbrook Rd. Wokgm —6C **36**
Emmbrook Vale. Wokgm —5C **36**
Emm Clo. Wokgm —6C **36**
Emmer Grn. Ct. Cav —5D **12**
Emmer Grn. Rd. Bin H —1G **13**
Emmview Clo. Wokgm —1C **46**
Empress Rd. Calc —1H **29**
Enborne Clo. Tile —4H **19**
Englefield Rd. Thea —2B **28**
Ennerdale Rd. Read —3E **33**
Enstone Rd. Wdly —4F **25**
Epping Clo. Read —5A **22**
Epsom Ct. Read —6A **22**
Erfstadt Ct. Wokgm —3F **47**

Erica Dri. Wokgm —3G **47**
Eric Av. Cav —4B **12**
Eriswell Clo. Lwr Ear —4D **34**
Erleigh Ct. Dri. Ear —5H **23**
Erleigh Ct. Gdns. Ear —5H **23**
Erleigh Rd. Read —6E **23**
Eskdale Rd. Winn —2F **35**
Eskin Clo. Tile —5D **20**
Essex St. Read —1C **32**
Essex Way. Son C —5F **5**
Eustace Cres. Wokgm —6G **37**
Evendon's Clo. Wokgm —5D **46**
Evendon's La. Wokgm —6B **46**
Evergreen Dri. Calc —2C **30**
Evergreen Way. Wokgm —3C **46**
Eversley Rd. Arbor X —6D **44**
Evesham Rd. Emm G —5C **12**
Exbourne Rd. Read —6D **32**
Exeter Ct. Read —6C **32**
Exeter Way. Thea —3D **28**
Exwick Sq. Read —6E **33**
Eynsford Clo. Cav —5F **13**
Eynsham Clo. Wdly —4D **24**

Faircross Rd. Read —1F **31**
Fairfield Rd. Gor —4D **48**
Fairford Rd. Tile —2H **19**
Fairlop Clo. Calc —2A **30**
Fairmead Rd. Shin —3F **43**
Fair Mile. Hen T —1A **2**
Fair Mile Ct. Hen T —2C **2**
Fairsted Clo. Tile —4C **20**
Fairview Av. Ear —6A **24**
Fairview Rd. Wokgm —3F **47**
Fairview Trading Est. Hen T —5E **3**
Fairwater Dri. Wdly —5B **24**
Fairway Av. Tile —6A **20**
Fakenham Clo. Lwr Ear —6H **33**
Falcon Av. Read —5F **33**
Falcon Way. Wokgm —2C **46**
Falkland Rd. Cav —2C **22**
Fallowfield Clo. Cav —6C **12**
Falmouth Rd. Read —1D **42**
Falstaff Av. Ear —4G **33**
Faringdon Wlk. Read —2E **31**
Farleigh M. Cav —5F **13**
Farman Clo. Wdly —4G **25**
Farm Clo. Pur T —5H **9**
Farm Cotts. Wokgm —6E **37**
Farm Dri. Tile —6G **19**
Farmers Clo. Read —2C **42**
Farmiloe Clo. Pur T —6H **9**
Farm Rd. Hen T —5E **3**
Farnham Dri. Cav —6F **13**
Farnsfield Clo. Lwr Ear —6H **33**
Farriers Clo. Wdly —5D **24**
Farrowdene Rd. Read —6D **32**
Fatherson Rd. Read —5E **23**
Fawcett Cres. Wdly —5C **24**
Fawley Rd. Read —1F **31**
Faygate Way. Lwr Ear —5A **34**
Fells, The. Tile —6F **19**
Felstead Clo. Ear —4G **33**
Felton Way. Tile —4H **19**
Fenchurch M. Winn —3F **35**
Fennel Clo. Ear —5G **33**
Fernbrook Rd. Cav —5H **11**
Fern Clo. Calc —1H **29**
Ferndale Av. Read —2D **30**
Ferndale Clo. Tile —1B **20**
Ferne Clo. Gor —4C **48**
Fern Glen. Tile —3H **19**
Fernhurst Rd. Calc —2H **29**
Fern Wlk. Calc —1H **29**
Ferry La. Gor —5B **48**
Ferry La. Warg —6D **6**
Fidlers Wlk. Warg —6F **7**
Field Clo. Bfld C —6G **39**

Field Rd. Read —6A **22**
Field View. Cav —1C **22**
Fieldway. Winn —4A **36**
Fife Ct. Read —4B **22**
Filbert Dri. Tile —4H **19**
Filey Rd. Read —5F **23**
Finbeck Way. Lwr Ear —6G **33**
Finch Rd. Ear —2B **34**
Finch Way. Bfld C —5G **39**
Fircroft Clo. Tile —3H **19**
Firmstone Clo. Lwr Ear —5B **34**
Fir Pit La. Tile —4H **19**
Fir's End. Bfld C —6F **39**
Firs La. Read —1G **31**
Firs Rd. Tile —6H **19**
Firs, The. Read —6A **22**
Fishers Ct. Emm G —4D **12**
Fishponds Clo. Wokgm —4D **46**
Fishponds Rd. Wokgm —4D **46**
Fitzroy Cres. Wdly —6F **25**
Five Acre. Tile —3G **19**
Flambards. Cav —2D **22**
Flamborough Clo. Lwr Ear —4D **34**
Flamborough Path. Lwr Ear
—4D **34**
Flamingo Clo. Wokgm —3B **46**
Flaxman Clo. Ear —4G **33**
Fleet Clo. Wokgm —2B **46**
Fleetham Gdns. Lwr Ear —5A **34**
Flodden Dri. Calc —2A **30**
Florence Ct. Read —6G **21**
Florence Wlk. Read —5E **23**
Florian Grdns. Read —1E **31**
(in two parts)
Florida Ct. Read —6H **21**
Flower's Hill. Pang —6B **8**
Fobney St. Read —6B **22**
Folly Grn. Woodc —3F **49**
Folly La. Bfld C —2F **39**
Folly Orchard Rd. Woodc —2F **49**
Fontwell Dri. Read —1C **30**
Forbury Ho. Read —5C **22**
Forbury Pk. Ind. Est. Read
—4D **22**
Forbury Rd. Read —4C **22**
(in two parts)
Forbury, The. Read —4C **22**
(in two parts)
Fordham Way. Lwr Ear —5B **34**
Forest Dean. Read —1D **42**
Forest Hill. Tile —2C **20**
Forest Rd. Wokgm & Binf —4D **36**
Forge Clo. Cav —2D **22**
Formby Clo. Ear —3D **34**
Forndon Clo. Lwr Ear —4D **34**
Fortrose Wlk. Calc —2B **30**
Fosters La. Wdly —6D **24**
Foundry Pl. Read —6B **22**
Fowler Clo. Ear —3H **33**
Fox Clo. Bfld C —6F **39**
Foxcombe Dri. Tile —5H **19**
Foxes Wlk. Charv —1F **25**
Foxglove Clo. Wokgm —1A **46**
Foxglove Gdns. Read —5H **21**
Foxhays Rd. Read —6E **33**
Foxhill Clo. Play —5H **13**
Fox Hill Ho. Read —1G **33**
Foxhill La. Play —3E **13**
Foxhill Rd. Read —6F **23**
Foxhunt Gro. Calc —2C **30**
Framlingham Dri. Cav —5F **13**
Frampton Clo. Wdly —3D **24**
Francis St. Read —6C **22**
Franklin Ct. Read —5A **22**
(off Franklin St.)
Franklin St. Read —5A **22**
Fraser Av. Cav —4D **12**
Frederick Pl. Wokgm —2D **46**

Freesia Clo. Wokgm —1A **46**
Frensham Grn. Read —5G **33**
Freshfield Clo. Ear —3D **34**
Freshwater Rd. Read —4F **23**
Friar St. Read —4B **22**
Friars Wlk. Read —4B **22**
Friday St. Hen T —3D **2**
Frieth Clo. Ear —5H **33**
Frilsham Rd. Read —2E **31**
Frimley Clo. Wdly —4C **24**
Fringford Clo. Lwr Ear —5B **34**
Frog Hall Dri. Wokgm —2H **47**
Frogmore Way. Read —1E **31**
Froxfield Av. Read —1H **31**
Fuchsia Clo. Calc —1H **29**
Fulford Way. Son C —2E **5**
Fullbrook Clo. Wokgm —5D **36**
Fullbrook Cres. Tile —1A **20**
Fuller's La. Graz —4E **41**
Fulmead Rd. Read —4F **21**
Fulmer Clo. Ear —4H **33**

Gainsborough Clo. Wdly —6F **25**
Gainsborough Cres. Hen T —5B **2**
Gainsborough Hill. Hen T —5C **2**
Gainsborough Rd. Hen T —5C **2**
Gainsborough Rd. Read —1E **31**
Gairn Clo. Tile —5D **20**
Gallowstree Rd. Pep C —2C **4**
Galsworthy Dri. Cav —5E **13**
Gap Way. Woodc —3F **49**
Gardens, The. S Sto —3C **48**
Garde Rd. Son —1D **24**
Garlands Clo. Bfld C —6E **39**
Garnet Hill. Read —6A **22**
Garnet St. Read —6B **22**
Garrard St. Read —4B **22**
(in two parts)
Garston Clo. Read —2D **30**
Garston Cres. Calc —1G **29**
Garston's Pk. Caravan Site. Tile
—6G **19**
Garth Clo. Winn —4H **35**
Gaskells End. Tok G —2G **11**
Gas Works Rd. Read —5D **22**
Gatcombe Clo. Calc —2H **29**
Gatehampton Rd. Gor —5C **48**
Gayhurst Clo. Cav —4E **13**
Gazelle Clo. Winn —3F **35**
Geoffreyson Rd. Cav —5G **11**
George St. Cav —3C **22**
George St. Read —4A **22**
Giffard Ho. Cav —3D **22**
Gifford Clo. Cav —5F **13**
Gillette Way. Read —4C **32**
Gillotts Clo. Hen T —5A **2**
Gillotts Hill. Harp —6B **2**
Gillott's La. Hen T —6A **2**
Gingells Farm Rd. Charv —5G **15**
Gipsy La. Ear —5C **34**
(in three parts)
Gipsy La. Tile —3B **20**
Gipsy La. Wokgm —3F **47**
Glade, The. Pur T —6H **9**
Gladridge Clo. Ear —2A **34**
Glamis Way. Calc —2G **29**
Glebelands Rd. Wokgm —1F **47**
Glebe La. Son —1D **24**
Glebe Ride. Gor —5B **48**
Glebe Rd. Pur T —5G **9**
Glebe Rd. Read —1D **32**
Glenbeigh Ter. Read —6H **21**
Glendevon Rd. Wdly —4E **25**
Gleneagles Ct. Read —5E **23**
(off Muirfield Clo.)
Glennon Clo. Read —2F **31**
Glenrhondda. Cav —5A **12**
Glenrosa Rd. Tile —4D **20**

Glenwood Dri. Tile —5H **19**
Gloucester Ct. Read —5G **21**
Gloucester Rd. Read —5G **21**
Glyme Wlk. Calc —3C **30**
Glyncastle. Cav —5A **12**
Goddard Clo. Shin —3F **43**
Goddard Ct. Winn —5G **35**
Godstow Clo. Wdly —4D **24**
(in two parts)
Goffs Hill. Cray P —6E **49**
Goldcrest Way. Tile —6G **19**
Goldsmid Rd. Read —5A **22**
Goldthorpe Gdns. Lwr Ear —6G **33**
Gooch Clo. Twy —1C **26**
Goodboys La. Graz —5C **40**
Goodchild Rd. Wokgm —2G **47**
Goodings Grn. Wokgm —2H **47**
Goodliffe Gdns. Tile —6H **9**
Goodrich Clo. Cav —5F **13**
Goodwin Clo. Calc —2B **30**
Goodwood Clo. Bfld C —6E **39**
Gordon Lodge. Read —5H **21**
Gordon Palmer Ct. Read —4F **21**
Gordon Pl. Read —4F **21**
Goring La. Bfld C —6H **39**
Goring Rd. Woodc —5E **49**
Gorrick Sq. Wokgm —5E **47**
Gorse Dri. Wdly —4F **25**
Gorselands. Cav —4B **12**
Gosbrook Houses. Cav —3D **22**
(off Star Rd.)
Gosbrook Rd. Cav —2B **22**
(in two parts)
Gosforth Clo. Lwr Ear —4B **34**
Gower St. Read —4H **21**
Graffham Clo. Lwr Ear —6A **34**
Grafton Clo. Tile —5A **20**
Graham Clo. Calc —2B **30**
Grahame Av. Pang —5C **8**
Granby Ct. Read —5F **23**
Granby End. Bfld C —5G **39**
Granby Gdns. Read —5F **23**
Grange Av. Read —6G **23**
Grange Av. Roth P —1F **5**
Grange Ct. Ear —4A **24**
Grangely Clo. Calc —2A **30**
Grange Rd. Hen T —4D **2**
Grantham Rd. Read —2C **30**
Granville Rd. Read —1D **30**
Grasmere Av. Tile —2C **20**
Grasmere Clo. Winn —5H **35**
Grass Hill. Cav —1H **21**
Gratton Rd. Read —6D **32**
Gratwicke Rd. Tile —4B **20**
Gravel Clo. Read —4A **12**
Gravel Hill. Hen T —3C **2**
Gravel Hill. Pep C —2E **5**
Gravel Hill Cres. Pep C —2E **5**
Gravelpithill La. Wokgm —3E **45**
Gravel Rd. Bin H —6G **13**
Graveney Dri. Cav —1H **21**
Gravett Clo. Hen T —5B **2**
Grayling Cl. Read —3B **22**
(off De Montfort Rd.)
Grays Cres. Wdly —5B **24**
Grazeley Rd. Three M —4B **42**
Gt. Auclum Pl. Bfld C —6G **39**
Gt. Knollys St. Read —4A **22**
Gt. Lea Cotts. Three M —3B **42**
Gt. Lea Ter. Three M —3B **42**
Greenacre Mt. Tile —4A **20**
Greenacres Av. Winn —3F **35**
Greenacres La. Winn —3F **35**
Green Croft. Wokgm —6H **37**
Greencroft Gdns. Read —1C **30**
Green Dean Hill. Tok G —6A **4**
Green Dri. Wokgm —4H **47**
Green End Clo. Spen W —6C **42**

Greenfields Rd. Read —6C **32**
Greenfinch Clo. Tile —6G **19**
Greenham Clo. Wdly —6F **25**
Green La. Bin H —1H **13**
Green La. Hen T —5C **2**
Green La. Hurst —3B **36**
Green La. Pang —6B **8**
Green La. Read —4D **30**
Green La. Son C —3E **5**
Green La. Uft N —6B **38**
Green La. Woodc —4G **49**
Greenleas Av. Emm G —3C **12**
Greenmoor. Woodc —4G **49**
Green Rd. Read —1G **33**
Greensward La. Arbor —5B **44**
Green, The. Thea —4B **28**
Green, The. Woos —1B **46**
Greenwood Gro. Winn —3A **36**
Greenwood Rd. Tile —1C **30**
Gregory Clo. Lwr Ear —6B **34**
Gresham Way. Read —2D **20**
Gresham Way Ind. Est. Tile
—2D **20**
Greyfriars Rd. Read —4B **22**
Grey's Ct. Read —5D **22**
Greys Hill. Hen T —4C **2**
Greys Rd. Hen T —5A **2**
Greystoke Rd. Cav —6D **12**
Grimmer Way. Woodc —3G **49**
Grosvenor Rd. Cav —1C **22**
Grove Cotts. Cav —5B **12**
Grove Hill. Cav —6B **12**
Groveland Pl. Read —4E **21**
Grovelands Av. Winn —4A **36**
Grovelands Clo. Winn —3A **36**
Grovelands Rd. Read —5E **21**
Grovelands Rd. Spen W —6D **42**
Grove Rd. Emm G —5B **12**
Grove Rd. Hen T —4D **2**
Grove Rd. Son C —4E **5**
Grove, The. Read —5D **22**
Grove, The. Twy —5A **16**
Gullane Ct. Read —5E **23**
(off Muirfield Clo.)
Gull Clo. Wokgm —3B **46**
Gun St. Read —5B **22**
Gurney Clo. Cav —5G **11**
Gurney Dri. Cav —6G **11**
Gwynne Clo. Tile —1A **20**

Haddon Dri. Wdly —4D **24**
Hadleigh Rise. Cav —5F **13**
Hadrian Wlk. E. Read —2D **32**
Hadrian Wlk. W. Read —2D **32**
Hafod. Cav —4A **12**
Hagbourne Clo. Woodc —3G **49**
Hagley Rd. Read —2C **32**
Halcyon Ter. Tile —4B **20**
Haldane Rd. Cav —5H **11**
Halfacre Clo. Spen W —5C **42**
Halls Rd. Shin —5F **33**
Hallsmead Ct. Read —3B **22**
(off Barton Rd.)
Halls Rd. Tile —6H **19**
Halpin Clo. Calc —2H **29**
Halstead Clo. Wdly —5D **24**
Hambleberry Ct. Tile —4H **19**
Hamble Ct. Read —4A **22**
Hambledon Clo. Lwr Ear —5D **34**
Hamilton Av. Hen T —4D **2**
Hamilton Rd. Read —5F **23**
Hamilton Rd. Warg —6F **7**
Hamlet, The. Gall C —3A **4**
Hampden Rd. Cav —2C **22**
Hampshire Wlk. Tile —6G **19**
(off Barton Rd.)
Hampshire Way. Wokgm —2A **46**
Hampstead Bottom. Son —2B **14**

Hampstead Ct. Read —4E **21**
Hampstead Hill. Son —2B **14**
Hampton Towers. Read —6H **21**
Hanbury Dri. Calc —2A **30**
Hanningtons Way. Bfld C —5H **39**
Hanover Ct. Cav —4D **12**
Hanwood Clo. Wdly —4B **24**
Harcourt Clo. Hen T —4B **2**
Harcourt Dri. Ear —4G **33**
Harding Rd. Wdly —4B **24**
Hardwick Rd. Tile —4C **20**
Hardwick Rd. Whit T —3B **8**
Hardy Clo. Cav —2D **22**
Harefield Clo. Winn —4H **35**
Hargreaves Wlk. Calc —2C **30**
Hargreaves Way. Calc —2C 30
  (off Bayford Dri.)
Harlech Av. Cav —5F **13**
Harley Rd. Cav —2C **22**
Harlton Clo. Lwr Ear —6B **34**
Harman Ct. Winn —4G **35**
Harmar Clo. Wokgm —2H **47**
Harness Clo. Read —2C **42**
Harpsden Rd. Hen T —5D **2**
Harpsden Way. Hen T —5D **2**
Harrier Clo. Wdly —6F **25**
Harrington Clo. Lwr Ear —4B **34**
Harris Arc. Read —4C **22**
Harris Clo. Wdly —4G **25**
Harrison Clo. Twy —1C **26**
Harrogate Rd. Cav —6H **11**
Harrow Ct. Read —6A **22**
Hart Dyke Clo. Wokgm —6E **47**
Hartigan Pl. Wdly —4F **25**
Hartland Rd. Read —5C **32**
Hartley Ct. Rd. Three M —2H **41**
Hartsbourne Rd. Ear —3G **33**
Harts Clo. Arbor —6D **44**
Hart's La. Uft N —3A **38**
Hartslock Ct. Pang —4A **8**
Hartslock Way. Tile —2H **19**
Hart St. Hen T —3D **2**
Hart St. Read —4H **21**
Harvard Clo. Wdly —4G **25**
Harvaston Pde. Tile —5C **20**
Harvest Clo. Tile —6G **19**
Harvey Ho. Read —6G **21**
Harwich Clo. Lwr Ear —5C **34**
Hastings Clo. Read —2D **30**
Hatch Ga. La. C Grn —1G **7**
Hatch Rd. Bfld —2A **40**
Hatchway. Read —1D **42**
Hatfield Ct. Calc —2G **29**
Hatford Rd. Read —2E **31**
Hatherley Rd. Read —6F **23**
Havelock Rd. Wokgm —2D **46**
Havelock St. Wokgm —2D **46**
Haven Rd. Read —5F **23**
Hawkchurch Rd. Read —6E **33**
Hawkedon Way. Lwr Ear —4C **34**
Hawker Way. Wdly —6F **25**
Hawkesbury Dri. Calc —3B **30**
Hawkes Clo. Wokgm —1D **46**
Hawkins Way. Wokgm —2D **46**
Hawksworth Rd. Bfld C —5G **39**
Hawley Clo. Calc —2H **29**
Hawthorn Cotts. Graz —5F **41**
Hawthorne Rd. Cav —6F **13**
Hawthornes. Tile —1G **19**
Hawthorn Gdns. Read —4F **33**
Hawthorns, The. Charv —1F **25**
Hawthorn Way. Son —2D **24**
Hayes La. Wokgm —4G **45**
Hayfield Clo. Tile —4H **19**
Hay Rd. Read —1A **32**
Haywards Clo. Hen T —4B **2**
Haywood Ct. Read —5G **23**
Haywood Way. Read —1C **30**
Hazel Clo. Bfld —3G **39**

Hazel Clo. Wokgm —3C **46**
Hazel Cres. Read —4F **33**
Hazel Dri. Wdly —1B **34**
Hazel Gdns. Son C —3E **5**
Hazelmoor La. Gall C —3B **4**
Hazel Rd. Pur T —5H **9**
Hazelwood Clo. Tile —3H **19**
Heacham Clo. Lwr Ear —6H **33**
Headington Clo. Wokgm —6G **37**
Headington Dri. Wokgm —6G **37**
Headley Clo. Wdly —4F **25**
Headley Pk. Ind. Est. Wdly —5E **25**
Headley Rd. Wdly —5D **24**
Headley Rd. E. Wdly —5E **25**
Hearn Rd. Wdly —1D **34**
Hearns La. Gall C —3B **4**
Heath Clo. Wokgm —4E **47**
Heath Croft. Cav —6C **12**
Heath Dri. Bin H —1H **13**
Heatherdene Clo. Read —1D **42**
Heathfield Av. Bin H —1A **14**
Heathfield Av. Tile —6A **20**
Heathfield Clo. Bin H —1A **14**
Heathlands Rd. Wokgm —5H **47**
Heath Rd. Read —1H **33**
Heathway. Tile —4H **19**
Heelas Rd. Wokgm —2D **46**
Helen Ct. Read —1D **30**
Hellas Rd. Wokgm —2D **46**
Helmsdale Clo. Read —4E **21**
Helston Gdns. Read —5C **32**
Hemdean Hill. Cav —1B **22**
Hemdean Rise. Cav —1B **22**
Hemdean Rd. Cav —2B **22**
Hengrove Clo. Lwr Ear —4D **34**
Henley Bri. Hen T —3D **2**
Henley Rd. Cav —1C **22**
Henley Rd. Warg —2D **6**
Henley Wood Rd. Ear —2C **34**
Henry St. Read —6C **22**
Herald Way. Wdly —5F **25**
Heritage Ct. Read —5A **22**
Hermes Clo. Wokgm —1G **45**
Hermitage Dri. Twy —5A **16**
Hermits Clo. Bfld C —5G **39**
Hermit's Hill. Bfld —4H **39**
Heroes Wlk. Read —1C **42**
Heron Dri. Twy —4B **16**
Heron Island. Cav —3D **22**
Heron Rd. Wokgm —2B **46**
Heron Shaw. Gor —4C **48**
Heron's Way. Wokgm —1H **47**
Heron Way. Read —2H **31**
Hertford Clo. Cav —4E **13**
Hertford Clo. Wokgm —3B **46**
Hewett Av. Cav —6G **11**
Hewett Clo. Cav —6G **11**
Hewgate Ct. Hen T —4D **2**
Hexham Rd. Read —3D **32**
Highbridge Clo. Cav —5F **13**
High Bri. Wharf. Read —5C **22**
Highbury Rd. Tile —5F **19**
Highdown Av. Cav —4B **12**
Highdown Hill Rd. Cav —3B **12**
Highfield. Lwr Ear —4A **34**
Highfield Clo. Wokgm —2F **47**
Highfield Ct. Bfld C —5G **39**
Highfield Ct. Twy —6B **16**
Highfield Rd. Tile —6G **9**
Highgate Rd. Wdly —1C **34**
Highgrove St. Read —1D **32**
Highgrove Ter. Read —6C **22**
Highland Av. Wokgm —3H **45**
Highmead Clo. Read —4F **33**
High Meadow. Cav —1G **21**
Highmoor Rd. Cav —1H **21**
High St. Goring, Gor —5B **48**
High St. Pangbourne, Pang —5B **8**
High St. Sonning, Son —1C **24**

High St. Streatley, Streat —5A **48**
High St. Theale, Thea —3D **28**
High St. Twyford, Twy —5A **16**
High St. Wargrave, Warg —1H **15**
High St. Whitchurch on Thames,
  Whit T —3B **8**
High Tree Dri. Ear —6A **24**
Highview. Calc —1G **29**
Highworth Way. Tile —2G **19**
Hilary Clo. Read —1D **42**
Hilbury Rd. Ear —3H **33**
Hilcot Rd. Read —4G **21**
Hildens Dri. Tile —5H **19**
Hillbrow. Read —5F **33**
Hillcrest La. Pep C —1E **5**
Hill Gdns. Streat —5A **48**
Hill Ho. Cav —6C **12**
Hill Lands. Warg —6E **7**
Hillside. Bfld C —5H **39**
Hillside. Ear —3C **34**
Hillside. Read —1D **32**
Hillside. Whit T —2C **8**
Hill St. Read —6C **22**
Hilltop Rd. Cav —5G **11**
Hilltop Rd. Ear —5A **24**
Hilltop Rd. Twy —3B **16**
Hilltopr Rd. Ear —4A **24**
Hillview Clo. Tile —2G **19**
Hilmanton. Lwr Ear —6G **33**
Hindhead Rd. Ear —3H **33**
Hinton Rd. Hurst —4C **26**
Hirstwood. Tile —3B **20**
Hirtes Av. Shin —3F **43**
Hocket, The. Hen T —2C **2**
Hodsoll Rd. Read —4A **22**
Hogarth Av. Read —1C **30**
Hogg Robinson Ho. Read —4B 22
  (off Greyfriars Rd.)
Hogmoor La. Hurst —3C **26**
Holberton Rd. Read —6E **33**
Holford Clo. Tile —4H **19**
Holkam Clo. Tile —3C **20**
Holland Rd. Tile —5A **20**
Hollicombe Clo. Read —5B **20**
Hollins Wlk. Read —6F **21**
Hollow La. Shin —2F **43**
Hollybush La. Bfld C —5D **38**
Hollydale Clo. Read —5F **33**
Hollym Clo. Lwr Ear —4D **34**
Holly Rd. Wdly —6F **25**
Holmedene. Bfld C —5G **39**
Holmemoor Dri. Son —2C **24**
Holme Pk. Farm La. Son —2B **24**
Holmes Clo. Wokgm —4D **46**
Holmes Cres. Wokgm —4C **46**
Holmes Rd. Read —1H **33**
Holmewood Clo. Wokgm —6D **46**
Holmlea Rd. Gor —6C **48**
Holmwood Av. Read —1C **30**
Holsworthy Clo. Lwr Ear —3D **34**
Holt La. Wokgm —1E **47**
Holt, The. Pur T —6A **10**
Holybrook Cres. Read —2D **30**
Holybrook Rd. Read —1A **32**
Holyrood Clo. Cav —4E **13**
Home Croft. Tile —3G **19**
Home Farm Clo. Read —3C **32**
Homestead, The. Bin H —1A **14**
Honey End La. Read —6D **20**
  (in two parts)
Honey Hill. Wokgm —6H **47**
Honiton Rd. Read —4D **32**
Hop Gdns. Hen T —2C **2**
Hornbeam Clo. Pur T —5H **9**
Hornbeam Clo. Wokgm —5A **46**
Horncastle Dri. Read —1C **30**
Hornsea Clo. Tile —3B **20**
Horse Clo., The. Cav —6D **12**
Horsepond Rd. Gall C —4A **4**

Horseshoe Cres. Bfld C —5F **39**
Horseshoe Pk. Pang —5C **8**
Horseshoe Rd. Pang —5C **8**
Hose Hill. Thea —6F **29**
Hosier St. Read —5B **22**
Howard Rd. Wokgm —3F **47**
Howard St. Read —5A **22**
Howth Dri. Wdly —5C **24**
Huckleberry Clo. Pur T —6H **9**
Hudson Rd. Wdly —1E **35**
Hughes Rd. Wokgm —1G **47**
Hugh Fraser Dri. Tile —6H **9**
Humber Clo. Wokgm —1B **46**
Hungerford Dri. Read —1H **31**
Hungerford La. Shur R —2F **27**
Hunters Chase. Cav —5H **11**
Hunters Hill. Bfld C —5E **39**
Hunters Way. Spen W —6C **42**
Huntingdon Clo. Lwr Ear —4D **34**
Huntingdonshire Clo. Wokgm
  —2A **46**
Huntley Ct. Read —6F **23**
Hurricane Way. Wdly —5F **25**
Hursley Clo. Tile —5B **20**
Hurst Pk. Rd. Twy —2B **26**
Hurst Rd. Twy —6B **16**
Huscarle Way. Tile —6H **9**
Hutsons Clo. Wokgm —6G **37**
Hutton Clo. Ear —4H **33**
Hyde End La. Three M —4C **42**
Hyde End Rd. Spen W & Shin
  —6C **42**
Hydes, The. Tile —6H **9**
Hyperion Way. Read —3C **32**

Ian Mikardo Way. Cav —2E **23**
Ibstock Clo. Read —5E **21**
Ibstone Av. Cav —5F **13**
Icknield Pl. Gor —3D **48**
Icknield Rd. Gor —3D **48**
Ilbury Clo. Shin —4F **43**
Ilchester M. Cav —4F **13**
Ilex Clo. Son C —4E **5**
Ilfracombe Way. Lwr Ear —3D **34**
Ilkley Rd. Cav —6H **11**
Illingworth Av. Cav —4F **13**
Ilsley Clo. Son C —3E **5**
Imperial Ct. Hen T —4D **2**
Imperial Way. Read —1B **42**
Inglewood Clo. Son C —3E **5**
Inglewood Ct. Read —6F **21**
Inkpen Clo. Read —2D **30**
Instow Rd. Ear —4A **34**
Invergordon Clo. Calc —2B **30**
Irainworth Clo. Lwr Ear —6H **33**
Iris Ct. Read —5B **20**
Irvine Way. Lwr Ear —6B **34**
Isis Clo. Winn —5G **35**
Isis Ct. Read —3C **22**
Island Farm Rd. Uft N —5C **38**
Island Rd. Read —4A **32**
Islandstone La. Hurst —6D **26**
Ivybank. Tile —3H **19**
Ivydene Rd. Read —3F **21**

Jacksons La. Cav —4F **11**
James Butcher Dri. Thea —3D **28**
James Ct. Read —1G **31**
James's La. Bfld —5C **40**
James St. Read —5A **22**
Janson Ct. Read —6A **22**
Japonica Clo. Wokgm —4A **46**
Jaques's La. Bfld C —2F **39**
Jasmine Clo. Wokgm —1A **46**
Jenner Wlk. Tile —5G 19
  (off Stratford Way)
Jerome Rd. Wdly —6C **24**

Jesse Ter. Read —5A **22**
Johannes Ct. Read —6G **21**
Jordan Clo. Cav —5F **13**
Jordan Clo. Spen W —6E **43**
Jordan's La. Bfld C —6E **39**
Josephine Ct. Read —6G **21**
Josey Clo. Son C —2E **5**
Jubilee Av. Wokgm —1D **46**
Jubilee Rd. Read —6H **23**
Jubilee Sq. Read —6C **22**
Julkes La. Arbor —1D **44**
Junction Rd. Read —6F **23**
Junipers, The. Wokgm —4A **46**
Juniper Way. Tile —2A **20**
Jupiter Way. Wokgm —2B **46**
Jutland Clo. Wokgm —2B **46**

Katesgrove La. Read —6B **22**
Kathleen Sanders Ct. Thea —2D **28**
Keane Clo. Wdly —4D **24**
Kearsley Rd. Read —6F **21**
Keats Clo. Wdly —2D **34**
Keats Rd. Wdly —2D **34**
Keephatch Rd. Wokgm —6H **37**
Kelburne Clo. Winn —3H **35**
Kelmscott Clo. Cav —2H **21**
Kelso M. Cav —4F **13**
Kelton Clo. Lwr Ear —4D **34**
Kelvedon Way. Cav —5H **11**
Kemble Ct. Calc —2A **30**
Kenavon Dri. Read —4D **22**
Kendal Av. Cav —5F **13**
Kendall Av. Shin —2F **43**
Kendrick Clo. Wokgm —3E **47**
Kendrick Ct. Read —6C **22**
Kendrick Rd. Read —6D **22**
Kenilworth Av. Read —1G **31**
Kennedy Dri. Pang —5C **8**
Kennedy Gdns. Ear —3A **34**
Kennet Ct. Wokgm —2C **46**
Kennet Pl. Bfld C —5G **39**
Kennet Side. Read —5C **22**
(in four parts)
Kennet St. Read —5D **22**
Kennylands Rd. Son C —4E **5**
Kensington Clo. Lwr Ear —5A **34**
Kensington Rd. Read —5G **21**
Kent Clo. Wokgm —3A **46**
Kentford Clo. Lwr Ear —4C **34**
Kenton Rd. Ear —2B **34**
Kenton's La. Up Cul —2D **6**
Kent Rd. Read —5G **21**
Kentwood Clo. Tile —3B **20**
Kentwood Hill. Tile —3B **20**
Kentwood Ho. Tile —3B **20**
Kentwood Ter. Tile —3B **20**
Kernham Dri. Tile —6H **9**
Kerris Way. Ear —5H **33**
Kesteven Way. Wokgm —2B **46**
Keston Clo. Cav —2D **22**
Kestrel Way. Read —2D **30**
Kestrel Way. Wokgm —2B **46**
Keswick Clo. Tile —5A **20**
Keswick Gdns. Wdly —1D **34**
Kettering Clo. Calc —2B **30**
Kew Ter. Tile —3B **20**
Kibblewhite Cres. Twy —4A **16**
Kidby's Ind. Est. Read —6B **22**
Kidmore End Rd. Emm G —1A **12**
Kidmore La. Kid E —5C **4**
Kidmore Rd. Cav —4H **11**
Kilburn Clo. Calc —2A **30**
Kildare Gdns. Cav —1D **22**
Kiln Brook Ho. Read —1B **32**
Kiln La. Spen W —6A **42**
Kiln La. Tile —4F **19**
Kiln Rd. Cav —4D **12**

Kilnsea Dri. Lwr Ear —4C **34**
Kiln View Rd. Read —4E **33**
Kilowna Clo. Charv —6F **15**
Kimberley Clo. Read —1H **31**
Kimpton Clo. Read —4E **33**
Kingfisher Ct. Twy —1B **26**
Kingfisher Dri. Wdly —6B **24**
Kingfisher Pl. Read —4C **22**
King James Way. Hen T —5B **2**
Kingsbridge Rd. Read —4D **32**
Kings Clo. Hen T —3C **2**
Kingsdown Clo. Ear —4A **34**
Kingsford Clo. Wdly —1F **35**
Kingsgate Pl. Read —5E 23
(off Kingsgate St.)
Kingsgate St. Read —5E **23**
Kingsley Clo. Charv —5F **15**
Kingsley Clo. Read —1C **42**
King's Meadow Rd. Read —4C **22**
Kings Reach Ct. Read —5C 22
(off Crane Wharf)
King's Rd. Cav —2C **22**
King's Rd. Hen T —3C **2**
King's Rd. Read —5C **22**
(in three parts)
Kingston Gdns. Read —4D **32**
Kingston La. Sul'd —2B **38**
King St. Read —5C **22**
King St. La. Winn —6G **35**
Kings Wlk. Hen T —2C **2**
King's Wlk. Read —5C **22**
Kingsway. Cav —4F **13**
Kingswood Ct. Read —6G **21**
Kinson Rd. Tile —3D **20**
Kintbury Wlk. Read —2F **31**
Kinver Wlk. Read —1C **32**
Kirkfell Clo. Tile —2H **19**
Kirkham Clo. Cav —4F **13**
Kirkstall Ct. Calc —2A **30**
Kirkwood Cres. Bfld C —5E **39**
Kirton Clo. Read —5E **21**
Kittiwake Clo. Wdly —5G **25**
Kitwood Dri. Lwr Ear —5D **34**
Knappe Clo. Hen T —5B **2**
Knapp, The. Ear —2A **34**
Knighton Clo. Cav —1B **22**
Knights Way. Emm G —5C **12**
Knollmead. Calc —2A **30**
Knoll, The. Tile —2G **19**
Knossington Clo. Lwr Ear —4B **34**
Knowle Clo. Cav —6G **11**
Knowle Rd. Wdly —2D **34**
Knowsley Rd. Tile —1G **19**

Laburnum Gdns. Read —5F **33**
Laburnum Rd. Winn —5H **35**
Lackmore Gdns. Woodc —3G **49**
Ladbroke Clo. Wdly —6E **25**
Lady Jane Ct. Cav —1C **22**
Ladymask Clo. Calc —2C **30**
Lakeside. Ear —3A **34**
Lalande Clo. Wokgm —2B **46**
Lambert Ct. Read —5C **20**
Lambfields. Thea —3C **28**
Lambourne Clo. Tile —4A **20**
Lambourne Gdns. Ear —2C **34**
Lambourne Rd. Son C —3D **4**
Lambridge La. Hen T —2A **2**
Lambridge Wood Rd. Hen T —1A **2**
Lambwoodhill. Graz —6G **41**
Lamerton Rd. Read —5D **32**
Lamorna Cres. Tile —3H **19**
Lamplighters Wlk. Calc —2C **30**
Lamsden Way. Bfld C —5G **39**
Lanark Clo. Wdly —6F **25**
Lancaster Clo. Read —1D **32**
Lancaster Gdns. Ear —3A **34**
Lancing Clo. Read —5G **21**

Landen Ct. Wokgm —4E **47**
Landrake Cres. Read —5D **32**
Lands End La. Land E —2G **25**
Lane End Clo. Shin —2F **43**
Langborough Rd. Wokgm —3F **47**
Langdale Gdns. Ear —4G **33**
Langford Clo. Cav —5D **12**
Langhams Way. Warg —6F **7**
Langley Comn. Rd. Arbor X &
    B'ham —6E **45**
Langley Hill. Tile —6H **19**
Langley Hill Clo. Tile —6H **19**
Langley La. Arbor —2C **44**
Laniver Clo. Ear —5A **34**
Lansdowne Rd. Tile —5H **19**
Lapwing Clo. Tile —6H **19**
Larch Av. Wokgm —1D **46**
Larch Clo. Bfld —4G **39**
Larch Dri. Wdly —1D **34**
Larchside Clo. Spen W —6C **42**
Lardon Cotts. Streat —5A **48**
Larissa Clo. Tile —3B **20**
Larks Meade. Ear —5H **33**
Larkspur Clo. Wokgm —1A **46**
Larkswood Clo. Tile —1A **20**
Lashbrook Mead. Lwr S —4C **6**
Lashbrook Rd. Lwr S —4C **6**
Latimer Dri. Calc —2H **29**
Latimer Rd. Wokgm —3E **47**
Laud's Clo. Hen T —4B **2**
Laud Way. Wokgm —2H **47**
Launceston Av. Cav —4F **13**
Launcestone Clo. Lwr Ear —4A **34**
Laurel Clo. Wokgm —3C **46**
Laurel Dri. Tile —4G **19**
Lavenham Dri. Wdly —4E **25**
Laverheath Rd. Lwr Ear —4D **34**
Lawnsend La. Charv —2G **25**
Lawns, The. Read —3E **33**
Lawrence Clo. Wokgm —2G **47**
Lawrence Rd. Tile —4D **20**
Layton Rise. Tile —1H **19**
Lea Clo. Read —3D **30**
Lea Rd. Son C —3E **5**
Leaver Rd. Hen T —4B **2**
Ledbury Clo. Read —4F **21**
Ledbury Dri. Calc —2A **30**
Ledran Clo. Lwr Ear —5B **34**
Leicester Clo. Hen T —2C **2**
Leighton Ct. Ear —3F **33**
Leiston Clo. Lwr Ear —5C **34**
Lemart Clo. Tile —4B **20**
Leney Clo. Wokgm —6G **37**
Lenham Clo. Winn —5B **36**
Lennox Clo. Calc —2G **29**
Lennox Rd. Read —1H **33**
Leonard Ct. Thea —3D **28**
Leopold Wlk. Read —5E **23**
Lesford Rd. Read —2H **31**
Lesley Ct. Read —6G **21**
Letcombe St. Read —5C **22**
Lexington Gro. Read —2D **42**
Leyburn Clo. Wdly —4F **25**
Leyland Gdns. Shin —2F **43**
Lichfield Clo. Lwr Ear —5B **34**
Lidstone Clo. Lwr Ear —5C **34**
Liebenrood Rd. Read —6F **21**
Lilac Clo. Pur T —5H **9**
Lilacs, The. Wokgm —4A **46**
Lilac Wlk. Calc —1H **29**
Lima Ct. Read —6A **22**
Lime Clo. Wokgm —3C **46**
Limetree Gro. Gor —5B **48**
Limmer Clo. Wokgm —4H **45**
Limmerhill Rd. Wokgm —3B **46**
Lincoln Clo. Winn —3F **35**
Lincoln Gdns. Twy —5A **16**
Lincoln Rd. Read —2D **32**
Lindberg Way. Wdly —3G **25**

Lind Clo. Ear —4A **34**
Linden Clo. Wokgm —3C **46**
Linden Hill La. Kiln G —1F **17**
Linden Rd. Read —4F **33**
Linden Rd. Wdly —2C **34**
Lindsey Clo. Wokgm —3B **46**
Linear Way. Calc —2H **29**
Lines Rd. Hurst —6B **26**
Lingholm Clo. Tile —1C **30**
Links Dri. Tile —4D **20**
Link Way. Arbor X —6D **44**
Linnet Clo. Tile —6G **19**
Linnet Wlk. Wokgm —2B **46**
Lismore Clo. Wdly —2D **34**
Lister Clo. Pur T —5H **9**
Littington Clo. Lwr Ear —6B **34**
Littlecote Dri. Read —6H **21**
Lit. Croft Rd. Gor —6C **48**
Lit. Glebe. Son —1D **24**
Lit. Heath Rd. Tile —5F **19**
Lit. Hill Rd. Hurst —2A **36**
Littlejohn's La. Read —4F **21**
(in two parts)
Lit. Oaks Dri. Tile —4H **19**
Littlestead Clo. Cav —4F **13**
Little St. Read —4H **21**
Liverpool Rd. Read —4F **23**
Livery Clo. Read —5C **22**
Livingstone Gdns. Wdly —1D **34**
Loader's La. Arbor —1D **44**
Lock Pl. Read —4E **23**
Lockstile Mead. Gor —4C **48**
Lockstile Way. Gor —5C **48**
Loddon Bri. Rd. Wdly —1E **35**
Loddon Dri. Warg —2F **15**
Loddon Hall Rd. Twy —4B **16**
Loddon Vale Cen. Wdly —5F **25**
Lodge Rd. Hurst —5B **26**
Logan Clo. Tile —5C **20**
Lomond Av. Cav —5F **13**
London Ct. Read —5C **22**
London Rd. Read —6D **22**
London Rd. Wokgm & Brack
    —2G **47**
London St. Read —5C **22**
London View. Twy —1B **26**
Longbarn La. Read —3C **32**
Longdon Rd. Winn —5G **35**
Longhurst Clo. Cav —1D **22**
Long La. Tile —3F **19**
Longleat Dri. Tile —1G **19**
Longmore Rd. Read —2E **43**
Longridge Clo. Read —5E **21**
Long's Way. Wokgm —1H **47**
Long Toll. Woodc & Whit H
    —4G **49**
Longworth Av. Tile —5G **19**
Lord Harris Ct. Sind —5F **35**
Lorne Pl. Read —5H **21**
Lorne St. Read —5H **21**
Lovatt Clo. Tile —5G **19**
Lovell Clo. Hen T —5B **2**
Loverock Rd. Read —3F **21**
Love's Clo. Bfld C —5F **39**
Lwr. Armour Rd. Tile —3A **20**
Lwr. Brook St. Read —6B **22**
Lwr. Earley Way. Lwr Ear —6A **34**
Lwr. Earley Way N. Winn —4E **35**
Lwr. Earley Way W. Read & Lwr Ear
    —1F **43**
Lwr. Elmstone Dri. Tile —3H **19**
Lwr. Field Rd. Read —6B **22**
Lwr. Henley Rd. Cav —2D **22**
Lwr. Meadow Rd. Read —4E **33**
Lwr. Mount. Read —1D **32**
Lowes Clo. S'lake —4C **6**
Lowestoft Clo. Lwr Ear —4C **34**
Lowfield Grn. Cav —6F **13**

Lowfield Rd. Cav —5D **12**
Low La. Calc —2C **30**
Lowther Clo. Wokgm —6C **36**
Lowther Rd. Wokgm —5B **36**
Loxwood. Ear —4B **34**
Lucey Clo. Tile —1G **19**
Luckley Path. Wokgm —2F **47**
Luckley Rd. Wokgm —5E **47**
Luckley Wood. Wokgm —5E **47**
Luckmore Dri. Ear —3H **33**
Luker Av. Hen T —2B **2**
Lulworth Rd. Read —6D **32**
Lunds Farm Rd. Wdly —4F **25**
Lundy La. Read —5F **21**
Luscombe Clo. Cav —2E **23**
Lutton Clo. Lwr Ear —6G **33**
Lycroft Clo. Gor —4C **48**
Lydford Rd. Read —1F **33**
Lyefield Ct. Emm G —4C **12**
Lyme Gro. Tile —3A **20**
Lymington Ga. Cav —5H **11**
Lynden M. Read —1C **32**
Lyndhurst Rd. Gor —5C **48**
Lyndhurst Rd. Tile —3C **20**
Lynmouth Ct. Read —3C **22**
Lynmouth Rd. Read —3B **22**
Lynton Clo. Wdly —1B **34**
Lyon Sq. Tile —4D **20**
Lysander Clo. Wdly —4F **25**
Lytham Clo. Read —2F **31**
Lytham End. Tile —1G **19**
Lytham Rd. Wdly —5D **24**

McCrae's Wlk. Warg —6E **7**
Mace Clo. Ear —5H **33**
Mackay Clo. Calc —3B **30**
McNair Clo. Lwr Ear —5H **33**
Macphail Clo. Wokgm —6H **37**
Magill Clo. Spen W —6C **42**
Magnolia Ct. Wdly —5F **25**
Magnolia Way. Wokgm —3C **46**
Magpie Way. Tile —6G **19**
Maiden Erlegh Dri. Ear —2A **34**
Maidenfield. Winn —4A **36**
Maiden La. Cen. Lwr Ear —5C **34**
Maiden Pl. Lwr Ear —4B **34**
Maitland Rd. Read —5H **21**
Maker Clo. Read —1E **31**
Makins Rd. Hen T —5A **2**
Maldon Clo. Read —6G **21**
Mallard Clo. Ear —3H **33**
Mallard Clo. Twy —1B **26**
Mallard Row. Read —6B **22**
Mallory Av. Cav —4E **13**
Malone Rd. Wdly —6C **24**
Maltby Way. Lwr Ear —6G **33**
Malthouse La. Read —4A **22**
Maltings Pl. Read —5B **22**
Malvern Clo. Wdly —6E **25**
Malvern Ct. Read —6E **23**
Malvern Way. Twy —3A **16**
Manchester Rd. Read —4F **23**
Mandela Ct. Read —5E **23**
Mander Ct. Cav —1C **22**
Mandeville Clo. Tile —1C **30**
Manea Clo. Lwr Ear —6B **34**
Manners Rd. Wdly —4C **24**
Mannock Way. Wdly —4G **25**
Manor Farm La. Tid —2B **18**
Manor Farm Rd. Read —4C **32**
Manor Ho. Ct. Read —1H **33**
Manor Pk. Clo. Tile —6H **19**
Manor Rd. Gor —5B **48**
Manor Rd. Hen T —5C **2**
Manor Rd. Whit T —3B **8**
Manor Rd. Wokgm —6D **46**
Manor Wood Ga. Lwr S —4B **6**

Mansell Ct. Read —4F **33**
Mansfield Hall. Read —6D **22**
Mansfield Rd. Read —6A **22**
Mansfield Rd. Wokgm —3C **46**
Man's Hill. Bfld C —5H **39**
Maple Bank. Rusc —4B **16**
Maple Clo. Son C —4F **5**
Maple Clo. Winn —3A 36
(off Meadow View)
Maple Ct. Gor —5B **48**
Mapledene. Cav —1H **21**
Mapledurham Dri. Pur T —5H **9**
Mapledurham View. Tile —2A **20**
Maple Gdns. Read —4F **33**
Marathon Clo. Wdly —4G **25**
Marchwood Av. Cav —2D **12**
Marcus Clo. Tile —5E **21**
Marefield. Lwr Ear —4B **34**
Marfleet Clo. Lwr Ear —4D **34**
Margaret Clo. Read —1D **42**
Maria Ct. Read —6G **21**
Markby Way. Lwr Ear —4C **34**
Market La. Hen T —3C **2**
Market Pl. Hen T —3C **2**
Market Pl. Read —5C **22**
Market Pl. Wokgm —2F **47**
Market Way. Read —5C **22**
Marks Rd. Wokgm —6D **36**
Marlborough Av. Read —1E **33**
Marlborough Cotts. Tile —3G **19**
Marlborough Ct. Read —6A **22**
Marlborough Ct. Wokgm —1G **47**
Marlborough Ho. Read —2E **33**
Marlborough Way. Calc —2G **29**
Marling Clo. Tile —2H **19**
Marlow Ct. Read —6E **23**
Marlow Rd. Hen T —2D **2**
Marmion Rd. Hen T —5D **2**
Marquis Pl. Read —5F **23**
Marsack St. Cav —2D **22**
Mars Clo. Wokgm —2B **46**
Marshall Clo. Pur T —6A **10**
Marshaw Ct. Read —3D **32**
Marsh Ct. Read —5G **21**
Marshland Sq. Emm G —5C **12**
Marsh La. Cav —1H **23**
Marten Pl. Tile —1H **19**
Martin Clo. Wdly —6D **24**
Martineaux La. Hurst —5B **26**
Martin's Dri. Wokgm —6E **37**
Mary Lyne Almshouses. Read
(off New La. Hill) —1C **30**
Mason St. Read —4H **21**
Master Clo. Wdly —4G **25**
Matlock Rd. Cav —6H **11**
Matson Dri. Rem —3E **3**
Matthewsgreen Rd. Wokgm
—6D **36**
Mattland Rd. Read —5H **21**
Mawbray Clo. Lwr Ear —4B **34**
Maxwell Clo. Wdly —4D **24**
Mayfair. Tile —5A **20**
Mayfield Av. Calc —2G **29**
Mayfield Dri. Cav —1E **23**
May Fields. Sind —5F **35**
Maying, The. Read —2C **42**
May Pk. Calc —2B **30**
Mays La. Ear —1A **34**
(in two parts)
May's Rd. Wokgm —2H **47**
Meachen Ct. Wokgm —2F **47**
Mead Clo. Tile —6G **19**
Meadow Clo. Gor —5C **48**
Meadowcroft Rd. Read —6D **32**
Meadow La. Pang —5C **8**
Meadow Rd. Ear —3C **34**
Meadow Rd. Hen T —4D **2**
Meadow Rd. Read —3A **22**
Meadow Rd. Wokgm —2D **46**

Meadowside Rd. Pang —5C **8**
Meadow View. Winn —3A **36**
Meadow Wlk. Wokgm —2D **46**
Meadow Way. Thea —3C **28**
Meadow Way. Wokgm —3D **46**
Meadway Precinct. Tile —6D **20**
Meadway, The. Tile —5B **20**
Mearings, The. Bfld —3C **40**
Measham Way. Lwr Ear —5B **34**
Meavy Gdns. Read —4C **32**
Medill Clo. Woodc —3F **49**
Medina Clo. Wokgm —1B **46**
Medway Clo. Wokgm —1B **46**
Melbourne Av. Winn —5H **35**
Meldreth Way. Lwr Ear —5B **34**
Melford Grn. Cav —4F **13**
Melksham Clo. Lwr Ear —6F **33**
Melling Clo. Ear —3D **34**
Mellor Wlk. Read —1C **32**
Melody Clo. Winn —3H **35**
Melrose Av. Read —1H **33**
Melrose Gdns. Arbor X —6D **44**
Memorial Av. S'lake X —1D **14**
Mendip Clo. Charv —6G **15**
Mendip Dri. Tile —6F **19**
Menpes Rd. Tile —6H **9**
Mentone Cotts. Wal L —5H **17**
Merchants Pl. Read —4B **22**
Mercury Av. Wokgm —2B **46**
Mereoak La. Graz —5H **41**
Merrivale Gdns. Read —5D **32**
Merryhill Chase. Winn —3H **35**
Merryhill Grn. La. Winn —3A **36**
Merton Rd. N. Read —5C **32**
Merton Rd. S. Read —5C **32**
Meteor Clo. Wdly —5F **25**
Metro Cen., The. Wokgm —4D **36**
Mews, The. Read —6F **23**
Mey Clo. Calc —1H **29**
Micklands Rd. Cav —6E **13**
Micro Cen., The. Read —3C **32**
Middlefields. Rusc —4B **16**
Middlefields Ct. Rusc —4B **16**
Midsummer Meadow. Cav —4A **12**
Mid Winter Clo. Tile —4B **20**
Mildenhall Clo. Lwr Ear —4C **34**
Milestone Av. Charv —6F **15**
Milestone Cres. Charv —6F **15**
Milestone Way. Cav —4E **13**
Miles Way. Wdly —5F **25**
Milford Rd. Read —3A **22**
Milkingbarn La. Shin —5H **43**
Millbank Cres. Wdly —6E **25**
Mill Clo. Wokgm —1C **46**
Milldown Av. Gor —4C **48**
Milldown Rd. Gor —4C **48**
Millenium Ct. Read —4C **32**
Millers Clo. Gor —4B **48**
Millers Gro. Calc —2B **30**
Milley La. Hare H —2D **16**
Milley Rd. Wal L —3G **17**
Mill Grn. Cav —3D **22**
(in two parts)
Mill La. Calc —3B **30**
Mill La. Ear —3D **34**
(in two parts)
Mill La. Hen T —5E **3**
Mill La. Read —5C **22**
(in two parts)
Mill La. S'lake —6A **6**
Mill La. Sind —5E **35**
Mill La. Tok G —1F **11**
Mill Mead. Wokgm —1D **46**
Mill Rd. Bfld —5B **30**
Mill Rd. Cav —3D **22**
Mill Rd. Gor —3C **48**
Mill Rd. Lwr S —6C **6**
Millworth La. Shin —4F **43**
Milman Rd. Read —1C **32**

Milsom Clo. Shin —3F **43**
Milton Clo. Hen T —4C **2**
Milton Ct. Wokgm —1E **47**
Milton Dri. Wokgm —1E **47**
Milton Gdns. Wokgm —2E **47**
Milton Rd. Ear —5H **23**
Milton Rd. Wokgm —6E **37**
Milton Way. Rusc —5C **16**
Minden Clo. Wokgm —2B **46**
Minerva Ho. Read —4C 22
(off Valpy St.)
Minster St. Read —5C **22**
Mint Clo. Ear —5G **33**
Minton Clo. Tile —4C **20**
Mire La. Wal L —5G **17**
Mitcham Clo. Read —1C **32**
Mitchell Way. Wdly —5G **25**
Mitford Clo. Read —6E **33**
Modbury Gdns. Read —4D **32**
Moffat Clo. Wdly —6F **25**
Mohawk Way. Wdly —4G **25**
Mole Rd. Sind —4E **45**
Moles Clo. Wokgm —3G **47**
Mollison Clo. Wdly —4G **25**
Molly Millars Bri. Wokgm —4E **47**
Molly Millars Clo. Wokgm —4E **47**
Molly Millar's La. Wokgm —3D **46**
Monarch Ho. Read —3B **22**
Monck Ct. Read —6G **21**
Monkley Ct. Cav —3D **22**
Monks Hood Clo. Wokgm —1H **47**
Monks Way. Read —1G **31**
Monmouth Ct. Read —4A **22**
(North St.)
Mons Clo. Wokgm —2B **46**
Montague St. Cav —2D **22**
Montague St. Read —5E **23**
Montgomery Dri. Spen W —6C **42**
Montpelier Dri. Cav —5E **13**
Montrose Wlk. Calc —2C **30**
Moor Copse Clo. Ear —3A **34**
Moores Grn. Wokgm —6H **37**
Moors Clo. Winn —3F 35
(off Ditchfield La.)
Moors, The. Pang —5C **8**
Morecambe Av. Cav —5H **11**
Moreleigh Clo. Read —6D **32**
Morgan Rd. Read —1D **32**
Moriston Clo. Read —4E **21**
Morlais. Cav —5B **12**
Morlands Av. Read —1D **30**
Morpeth Clo. Read —2D **32**
Morriss Ct. Read —5E 23
(off Orts Rd.)
Mortimer Clo. Read —1D **42**
Morton Ct. Read —1E **33**
Morton Pl. Thea —2D **28**
Moss Clo. Cav —1D **22**
Mountfield. Gor —4C **48**
Mt. Pleasant. Read —6C **22**
Mt. Pleasant. Wokgm —2D **46**
Mt. Pleasant Gro. Read —6C **22**
Mount St. Read —1C **32**
(in two parts)
Mount, The. Cav —1A **22**
Mount, The. Read —1E **33**
Mt. View. Hen T —3C **2**
Mowbray Dri. Tile —4D **20**
Mower Clo. Wokgm —1H **47**
Mowforth Clo. Woodc —2F **49**
Muirfield Clo. Read —5E **23**
Mulberry Bus. Pk. Wokgm —4D **46**
Mulberry Clo. Wdly —6D **24**
Mulberry Clo. Wokgm —2F **47**
Mulberry Way. Thea —3D **28**
Mullens Ter. Chaz H —2G **11**
Mumbery Hill. Warg —1B **16**

Mundesley St. Read —6C 22
(off Southampton St.)
Munro Av. Wdly —2E 35
Murdoch Rd. Wokgm —3F 47
Murray Rd. Wokgm —2D 46
Mustard La. Son —3D 24
Muswell Clo. Thea —3D 28
Mylne Sq. Wokgm —2G 47
Myrtle Clo. Bfld C —5G 39
Myrtle Clo. Tile —1H 19
Myton Wlk. Thea —3D 28

Nabbs Hill Clo. Tile —1H 29
Napier Ct. Trading Est. Read
—4C 22
Napier Rd. Read —4C 22
Narromine Dri. Calc —2C 30
Nash Clo. Ear —3H 33
Nash Gro. La. Wokgm —6B 46
Nashgrove Ride. Wokgm —6H 45
Neath Gdns. Tile —5C 20
Nelson Rd. Cav —2D 22
Nelson's La. Hurst —1E 37
Neptune Clo. Wokgm —2B 46
Netley Clo. Cav —4F 13
Nevis Rd. Tile —1A 20
Newalls Rise. Warg —6F 7
Newark St. Read —6C 22
New Bath Rd. Charv —5G 15
Newbery Clo. Tile —3A 20
New Bright St. Read —6B 22
Newcastle Rd. Read —2D 32
Newell's La. Cav —4E 11
Newfield Rd. Son C —2E 5
New Hill. Pur T —5H 9
Newlands Av. Cav —1C 22
Newlands Cotts. Wokgm —1E 45
New La. Hill. Tile —5B 20
Newlyn Gdns. Read —5C 32
Newmarket Clo. Lwr Ear —4C 34
Newport Rd. Read —3B 22
New Rd. Bfld C —6B 40
New Rd. Read —1E 33
New Rd. Rusc —4C 16
New Rd. S'lake —6A 6
New Rd. Twy —3A 16
New St. Hen T —3D 2
Newton Av. Cav —5E 13
Newtown Gdns. Hen T —5D 2
Newtown Rd. Hen T —5E 3
Niagara Rd. Hen T —5D 2
Nicholas Rd. Read —5A 22
(off Prospect St.)
Nicholas Rd. Hen T —5A 2
Nightingale Rd. Wdly —1H 34
Nimrod Clo. Wdly —5G 25
Nimrod Way. Read —1C 32
Nonsuch Clo. Wokgm —1E 47
Norcot Rd. Tile —4B 20
Nores Rd. Read —1E 43
Norfolk Clo. Wokgm —2B 46
Norfolk Rd. Read —5F 21
Norman Av. Hen T —4D 2
Norman Rd. Cav —6D 12
Normanstead Rd. Tile —4H 19
Norreys Av. Wokgm —2G 47
Norris Grn. Land E —3F 25
Norris Rd. Read —6H 23
Northbourne Clo. Lwr Ear —4A 34
Northam Clo. Lwr Ear —3D 34
Northbrook Rd. Cav —5E 13
Northbury Av. Rusc —4B 16
Northbury Rd. Rusc —4B 16
Northcourt Av. Read —2E 33
North Dri. Sul'd —1C 38
Northfield Av. Lwr S —4B 6
Northfield Clo. Hen T —2C 2
(off Badgemore La.)

Northfield Cotts. Read —3B 22
Northfield End. Hen T —2C 2
Northfield Rd. Lwr S —4C 6
Northfield Rd. Read —3B 22
North St. Cav —2C 22
North St. Read —4A 22
Northumberland Av. Read —2D 32
North Wlk. Thea —2D 28
North Way. Wokgm —1A 46
Norton Rd. Read —5F 23
Norton Rd. Wokgm —3F 47
Norton Rd. Wdly —1E 35
Norwich Dri. Wdly —4B 24
Norwood Rd. Read —5E 23
Notton Way. Lwr Ear —6G 33
Nunhide La. Sul —3E 19
Nun's Acre. Gor —4B 48
Nursery Gdns. Pur T —5G 9
Nuthatch Dri. Ear —2A 34
Nut La. Wal L —4H 17
Nutmeg Clo. Ear —5G 33

Oakdale Clo. Tile —4H 19
Oakdale Way. Wdly —4F 25
Oakdene. Bfld C —6F 39
Oakdene. Woodc —4G 49
Oak Dri. Bfld C —6E 39
Oak Dri. Wdly —6F 25
Oak Grn. Read —6E 33
Oakham Clo. Tile —2A 20
Oaklands. Read —6F 23
(in two parts)
Oaklands Bus. Pk. Wokgm —5C 46
Oaklands Dri. Wokgm —4C 46
Oaklands Pk. Wokgm —4D 46
Oakley Rd. Cav —6A 12
Oakside Way. Shin —6F 33
Oaks Rd. S'lake —4B 6
Oak Tree Copse. Tile —1B 20
Oak Tree Rd. Tile —2A 20
Oakstow Rd. Tile —5A 10
Oak View. Tile —4H 19
Oak Way. Wdly —2C 34
Oatlands Rd. Shin —3G 43
Oban Gdns. Wdly —2D 34
Odell Clo. Lwr Ear —6A 34
Odiham Av. Cav —5F 13
Ogmore Clo. Tile —5B 20
Old Acres La. Charv —5G 15
Old Barn Clo. Cav —4B 12
Old Bath Rd. Calc —2H 29
Old Bath Rd. Charv —6F 15
(in two parts)
Old Bath Rd. Son —3B 24
(in two parts)
Old Copse Gdns. Son C —2E 5
Old John St. Tile —5A 20
Old Farm Cres. Tile —2H 19
Oldfield Clo. Ear —5A 24
Old Forest Rd. Wokgm —6B 36
Old Kennel's Ct. Read —1D 30
Old La., The. Read —1A 32
Old Orchard, The. Calc —2B 30
Old Well Ct. Son —6C 14
Old Whitley Wood La. Read
—2D 42
Old Woosehill La. Wokgm —1C 46
Oliver Dri. Calc —1G 29
Olivia Ct. Wokgm —2E 47
Omer's Rise. Bfld C —5E 39
Onslow Gdns. Cav —1D 22
Opal Way. Wokgm —1B 46
Orchard Av. Son C —3D 4
Orchard Chase. Read —5C 26
Orchard Clo. Hen T —5D 2
Orchard Clo. S'lake —6A 6
Orchard Clo. Spen W —6C 42
Orchard Clo. Tile —6G 9

Orchard Clo. Wokgm —2G 47
Orchard Ct. Read —1D 42
Orchard Est. Twy —5B 16
Orchard Field. Gall C —3B 4
Orchard Gro. Cav —6F 13
Orchard Pl. Wokgm —2F 47
Orchard Rd. Hurst —5C 26
Orchard St. Read —6C 22
Orchard, The. Thea —2D 28
Oregon Av. Tile —1A 20
Orkney Clo. Calc —2B 30
Ormonde Rd. Wokgm —3D 46
Ormsby St. Read —5H 21
Orrin Clo. Tile —5E 21
Orts Rd. Read —5D 22
(in two parts)
Orville Clo. Wdly —5F 25
Orwell Clo. Cav —6A 12
Osborne Rd. Read —4E 21
Osborne Rd. Wokgm —2F 47
Osprey Ct. Read —5D 22
Osterley Clo. Wokgm —3H 47
Osterley Dri. Cav —4F 13
Overbury Av. Wokgm —5C 36
Overdown Rd. Tile —2H 19
Overlanders End. Tile —1B 20
Owl Clo. Wokgm —3B 46
Owston. Lwr Ear —4B 34
Oxford Rd. Tile & Read —5H 9
Oxford Rd. Wokgm —2E 47
Oxford Rd. Woodc —2F 49
Oxford St. Cav —2B 22

Pacific Ho. Read —6B 32
Pack & Prime La. Hen T —4A 2
Paddick Clo. Son —1D 24
Paddock Heights. Twy —6B 16
Paddock Rd. Cav —3E 23
Padley Ct. Read —5D 22
(off Dell, The)
Padstow Gdns. Read —5C 32
Page's Croft. Wokgm —3G 47
Pages Orchard. Son C —3D 4
Paice Grn. Wokgm —1G 47
Palmera Av. Calc —2H 29
Palmer Ct. Wokgm —2F 47
Palmer Pk. Av. Read —6G 23
Palmer School Rd. Wokgm —2F 47
Palmer's La. Bfld C —6F 39
Palmer's La. Graz —5D 40
Palmerstone Rd. Ear —5H 23
Pangbourne Hill. Pang —5A 8
Pangbourne Rd. Thea & Tid
—4B 28
Pangbourne St. Read —4E 21
Paprika Clo. Ear —5G 33
Parade, The. Read —2G 31
Parade, The. Wdly —2D 34
Paradise M. Hen T —3C 2
Paradise Rd. Hen T —4C 2
Park Av. Wokgm —3E 47
(in two parts)
Park Clo. Son C —2F 5
Parkcorner La. Wokgm —2E 45
Park Cres. Read —6E 21
Park Gro. Read —6E 21
Parkhill Dri. Tile —2A 20
Parkhouse La. Read —6G 21
Park La. Charv —6F 15
Park La. Tile —6H 19
Park Rd. Hen T —4D 2
Park Rd. Wokgm —2E 47
Parkside. Hen T —3B 2
Parkside Rd. Read —6G 21
Park View Dri. N. Charv —5F 15
Park View Dri. S. Charv —5F 15
Park Wlk. Pur T —5A 10
(in two parts)

Parkway Dri. Son —1D 24
Parsley Clo. Ear —5G 33
Parthia Clo. Read —6C 22
Partridge Dri. Tile —6G 19
Pasture Clo. Lwr Ear —6A 34
Patrick Rd. Cav —2C 22
Patriot Pl. Read —5D 22
Patten Ash Dri. Wokgm —1H 47
Pattinson Rd. Read —2E 43
Pavenham Clo. Lwr Ear —6A 34
Payley Dri. Wokgm —6H 37
Peach St. Wokgm —2F 47
Peacock Wlk. Wokgm —3B 46
Pearces Orchard. Hen T —2C 2
Pearman's Glade. Read —6F 33
Pearman's La. Lwr Ear —1G 43
(in two parts)
Pearson Rd. Son —1C 24
Pearson Way. Wdly —1D 34
Peel Clo. Cav —2E 23
Peel Clo. Wdly —4G 25
Pegasus Ct. Tile —5H 9
Peg's Grn. Clo. Read —6E 21
Pelham Ct. Read —6G 21
Pell St. Read —6C 22
Pemberton Gdns. Calc —2A 30
Pembroke Clo. Bfld C —5H 39
Pembroke Ho. Cav —3D 22
Pembroke Pl. Cav —1D 22
Pendennis Av. Cav —4F 13
Pendragon Ct. Read —1G 31
Pendred Rd. Read —2E 43
Penn Clo. Cav —4B 12
Pennfields. Rusc —4B 16
Pennine Clo. Tile —6G 19
Pennine Way. Charv —6G 15
Penny Piece. Gor —4C 48
Pennyroyal Ct. Read —6B 22
Penny's La. C Grn —2E 7
Penroath Av. Read —6F 21
Penrose Av. Wdly —6D 24
Pentland Clo. Read —1C 30
Pentridge Ho. Read —6D 32
Peppard Hill. Roth P —1E 5
Peppard La. Hen T —6C 2
Peppard Rd. Cav —1C 22
Peppard Rd. Son C —2E 5
Pepper La. Ear —2F 33
Peregrine Clo. Wokgm —3C 46
Periam Clo. Hen T —5B 2
Perimeter Rd. Wdly —4F 25
Perkins Way. Wokgm —3D 46
Perth Clo. Wdly —3F 25
Petrel Clo. Wokgm —3B 46
Petworth Av. Read —3C 30
Petworth Ct. Read —6H 21
Pevensey Av. Cav —5F 13
Pheasant Clo. Winn —4H 35
Phillimore Rd. Cav —2D 12
Phillips Clo. Wdly —3G 25
Phoebe Ct. Read —6B 22
Phoenix Clo. Wokgm —2B 46
Phyllis Ct. Dri. Hen T —2D 2
Pickwell Clo. Lwr Ear —5B 34
Picton Way. Lwr Ear —6C 12
Pierce Field. Calc —2H 29
Pierce's Hill. Tile —3H 19
Piggott's Rd. Cav —3D 22
Pightle, The. Graz —5C 40
Pigott Rd. Wokgm —6G 37
Pikeshaw Way. Tile —2H 19
Pimento Dri. Ear —5G 33
Pincents Kiln Trading Est. Tile
—2F 29
Pincents La. Tile —2E 29
Pinchcut. Bfld C —5F 39
Pine Croft Rd. Wokgm —6D 46
Pine Gro. Twy —5A 16
Pine Ridge Rd. Bfld C —5F 39

Pine Tree Ct. Emm G —5B **12**
Pingewood Rd. Ping —6C **30**
Pitcroft Av. Read —6H **23**
Pitford Rd. Wdly —4F **25**
Pitts La. Ear —5A **24**
Players Grn. Wdly —1D **34**
Playhatch Rd. Play —5H **13**
Play Platt. Thea —2C **28**
Play Platt Houses. Thea —2C **28**
Plough La. S'lake —1C **14**
Plough La. Wokgm —1H **47**
Plover Clo. Wokgm —3C **46**
Plowden Way. S'lake X —1D **14**
Plummery, The. Read —5D 22
(off Blakes Cotts.)
Plumtrees. Ear —4A **34**
Plymouth Av. Wdly —1B **34**
Plympton Clo. Ear —3D **34**
Polehampton Clo. Twy —6A **16**
Polehampton Ct. Twy —6A **16**
Pollards Way. Calc —2H **29**
Polsted Rd. Tile —3A **20**
Pond End Rd. Son C —2F **5**
Pond Head La. Ear —2C **34**
Pond La. Map —3C **10**
Poole Clo. Tile —5C **20**
Poplar Av. Tile —1C **20**
Poplar Gdns. Read —5F **33**
Poplar La. Hurst —3C **26**
Poplar La. Winn —3A **36**
Poppy Pl. Wokgm —2E **47**
Poppy Way. Calc —1H **29**
Porchfield Clo. Ear —5H **33**
Porlock Pl. Calc —2G **29**
Porter Clo. Lwr Ear —6B **34**
Portland Gdns. Tile —5H **19**
Portman Rd. Read —3E **21**
Portmeirion Gdns. Tile —3C **20**
Portrush Clo. Wdly —6C **24**
Portway Clo. Read —6H **21**
Post Horn Pl. Calc —2C **30**
Potkiln La. Woodc —5F **49**
Pottery Rd. Tile —3C **20**
Poundfield Way. Twy —1C **26**
Pound La. Hurst —1D **36**
Pound La. Son —2D **24**
Precinct, The. Cav —5D **12**
Preston Rd. Read —1C **32**
Priest Av. Wokgm —3H **47**
Priest Hill. Cav —1B **22**
Primrose Clo. Pur T —5H **9**
Primrose La. Winn —3H **35**
Prince of Wales Av. Read —5G **21**
Prince's St. Read —5D **22**
Prince William Dri. Tile —3H **19**
Priory Av. Cav —2B **22**
Priory Copse. Pep C —2E **5**
Priory Ct. Winn —3H **35**
Priory, The. Winn —3H **35**
Proctors Rd. Wokgm —2H **47**
Promenade Rd. Cav —2B **22**
Prospect Ct. Read —6E **21**
Prospect St. Cav —2B **22**
Prospect St. Read —5A **22**
Pudding La. Arbor —5C **44**
Pump La. Graz —5F **41**
Purbeck Ho. Read —6D **32**
Purfield Dri. Warg —6F **7**
Purley La. Pur T —5H **9**
Purley Village. Pur T —5H **9**
Purley Way. Pang —5D **8**
Purslane. Wokgm —3G **47**
Putman Pl. Hen T —4D **2**

Quantock Av. Cav —5E **13**
Quantock Clo. Charv —6G **15**
Quartz Clo. Wokgm —1A **46**
Quebec Rd. Hen T —5D **2**

Queen Anne's Ga. Cav —2D **22**
Queen Clo. Hen T —4D **2**
Queensborough Dri. Cav —5H **11**
Queen's Cotts. Read —5C **22**
Queen's Dri., The. Ear —2F **33**
Queens Lawns. Read —6E **23**
Queen's Rd. Cav —3C **22**
Queen's Rd. Read —5C **22**
(in two parts)
Queen St. Cav —1B **22**
Queen St. Hen T —4D **2**
Queens Wlk. Read —5B **22**
Queensway. Cav —4E **13**
Queen Victoria St. Read —4C **22**
Quentin Rd. Wdly —6C **24**

Radbourne Rd. Calc —2A **30**
Radcot Clo. Wdly —3D **24**
Radnor Clo. Hen T —3D **2**
Radnor Rd. Ear —3B **34**
Radstock La. Ear —3H **33**
Radstock Rd. Read —5F **23**
Ragdale. Bfld C —5F **39**
Raggleswood Clo. Ear —3B **34**
Raglan Ct. Read —4E **33**
Raglan Gdns. Cav —6D **12**
Ragley M. Cav —4E **13**
Railton Clo. Read —1E **43**
Railway Cotts. Gor —5C **48**
Railway Cotts. Graz —5F **41**
Ramsbury Dri. Ear —2H **33**
Rances La. Wokgm —3H **47**
Randolph Rd. Read —3B **22**
Rangewood Av. Read —3C **30**
Ratby Clo. Lwr Ear —4B **34**
Ravenglass Clo. Lwr Ear —3B **34**
Ravensbourne Dri. Wdly —4D **24**
Ravenscroft Rd. Hen T —3C **2**
Rawling Clo. Read —1D **42**
Rayleigh Clo. Wdly —1D **34**
Reade's La. Gall C —3B **4**
Reading Link Retail Pk. Read
—1B **32**
Reading Retail Pk. Read —3E **21**
Reading Rd. Arbor —4A **44**
Reading Rd. Bfld —3A **40**
Reading Rd. Gor —5C **48**
Reading Rd. Hen T —4D **2**
Reading Rd. Pang —5C **8**
Reading Rd. Streat —5A **48**
Reading Rd. Winn & Wokgm
—4H **35**
Reading Rd. Woodc —2G **49**
Reading Rd. Wdly —4B **24**
Reckitt Ho. Read —4F **33**
Recreation La. Spen W —6C **42**
Recreation Rd. Bfld C —6F **39**
Recreation Rd. Tile —4B **20**
Recreation Rd. Warg —6F **7**
Rectory Clo. Wokgm —2F **47**
Rectory Rd. Cav —2B **22**
Rectory Rd. Streat —3A **48**
Rectory Rd. Wokgm —2F **47**
Redberry Clo. Cav —5E **13**
Red Cottage Dri. Calc —2H **29**
Red Cross Rd. Gor —5C **48**
Redhatch Dri. Ear —4G **33**
Redhouse Clo. Lwr Ear —6A **34**
Red Ho. Dri. Son C —3F **5**
Redlands Rd. Read —6D **22**
Red La. Woodc —1E **49**
Redlane Ct. Read —1E **33**
Redruth Gdns. Read —5C **32**
Redwood Av. Wdly —1F **35**
Redwood Way. Tile —1A **20**
Reeds Av. Ear —3G **33**
Reeves Way. Wokgm —4D **46**
Regency Heights. Cav —6H **11**

Regent Clo. Lwr Ear —5B **34**
Regent Ct. Read —4B **22**
Regents Ga. Read —6C **22**
Regent St. Read —5F **23**
Regis Clo. Read —1E **43**
Rembrandt Clo. Wokgm —2A **46**
Rembrandt Way. Read —1H **31**
Remenham Chu. La. Rem —1F **3**
Remenham La. Rem —3E **3**
Renault Rd. Wdly —6F **25**
Repton Rd. Ear —3B **34**
Restwold Clo. Read —2F **31**
Retford Clo. Wdly —3E **25**
Reynards Clo. Winn —4H **35**
Rhigos. Cav —4A **12**
Rhodes Clo. Ear —3D **34**
Ribbleton Clo. Ear —3D **34**
Richard Nevill Ct. Cav —2D 22
(off Nelson Rd.)
Richborough Clo. Lwr Ear —4A **34**
Richfield Av. Read —3H **21**
Richmond Rise. Wokgm —1B **46**
Richmond Rd. Cav —6H **11**
Richmond Rd. Read —4G **21**
Rickman Clo. Wdly —1C **34**
Rider's La. Graz —2D **40**
Ridge Hall Clo. Cav —1H **21**
Ridgemount Clo. Tile —2G **19**
Ridge Way. Warg —6E **7**
Ridgeway, The. Cav —1C **22**
Ridgeway, The. Wdly —1E **35**
Ridings, The. Emm G —2D **12**
Riding Way. Wokgm —2A **46**
Ridlington Clo. Lwr Ear —4D **34**
Riley Rd. Tile —4C **20**
Ringwood Rd. Tile —3D **20**
Ripley Rd. Tile —3D **20**
Rise, The. Cav —6C **12**
Rissington Clo. Tile —1B **20**
Riverdene Dri. Winn —3E **35**
River Gdns. Pur T —5A **10**
Rivermead Rd. Wdly —1E **35**
River Rd. Cav —1G **21**
River Rd. Read —6B **22**
Riversdale Ct. Read —4F **23**
Riverside Caravan Pk. Read
—2D **20**
Riverside Ct. Cav —2B **22**
River Ter. Hen T —3D **2**
Riverview Rd. Pang —4B **8**
River Yd. Twy —5H **15**
Roberts Gro. Wokgm —4C **46**
Robin Clo. Bfld C —5G **39**
Robindale Av. Ear —3C **34**
Robin Hood La. Winn —4H **35**
Robin Hood Way. Winn —3H **35**
Robin Way. Tile —6G **19**
Rochester Av. Wdly —3D **24**
Rockbourne Gdns. Tile —3D **20**
Rodney Ct. Read —6B **22**
Rodway Rd. Tile —2D **20**
Rokeby Dri. Tok G —2F **11**
Rollington Clo. Lwr Ear —4D **34**
Roman Way. Ear —3C **34**
Romany Clo. Tile —3D **20**
Romany La. Tile —4C **20**
(in two parts)
Romsey Clo. Ear —3D **34**
Romsey Rd. Tile —3D **20**
Rona Ct. Read —4E **21**
Rook Clo. Wokgm —3B **46**
Rosebay. Wokgm —6H **37**
Rosebery Rd. Tok G —3G **11**
Rose Clo. Wdly —5G **25**
Rose Ct. Wokgm —2F **47**
Rosecroft Way. Shin —3F **43**
Rosedale Cres. Ear —4H **23**
Rose Gdns. Wokgm —2F **47**
Rosehill Houses. Cav —3D **12**

Rosehill Pk. Cav —3C **12**
Rose Kiln La. Read —6B **22**
Rose La. C Grn —1H **7**
Rosemary Av. Ear —5G **33**
Rosemead Av. Tile —1G **19**
Rose St. Wokgm —2F **47**
Rose Wlk. Read —5B **22**
Rosewood. Wdly —1C **34**
Roslyn Rd. Wdly —6C **24**
Rossendale Rd. Cav —1E **23**
Rossington Pl. Read —6D **32**
Ross Rd. Read —3B **22**
Rotherfield Av. Wokgm —1C **46**
Rotherfield Clo. Thea —2E **29**
Rotherfield Rd. Hen T —6C **2**
Rotherfield Way. Cav —6B **12**
Rothwell Gdns. Wdly —3E **25**
Rothwell Wlk. Cav —2E **23**
Roundabout La. Winn —6A **36**
Roundhead Rd. Thea —2C **28**
Routh La. Tile —6B **20**
Rowallan Clo. Cav —4E **13**
Rowan Clo. Son C —4E **5**
Rowan Clo. Wokgm —3C **46**
Rowan Dri. Wdly —4D **24**
Rowan Way. Bfld —4G **39**
Rowe Ct. Read —4E **21**
Rowland Way. Ear —4G **33**
Row La. D'den —2F **13**
Rowley Rd. Read —2C **32**
Royal Av. Calc —2G **29**
Royal Ct. Read —5D **22**
Royal Mans. Hen T —4D **2**
Royal Sta. Ct. Twy —6A **16**
Royston Clo. Tile —5C **20**
Ruby Clo. Wokgm —1A **46**
Rupert Clo. Hen T —2D **2**
Ruperts La. Hen T —2D **2**
Rupert Sq. Read —5E **23**
Rupert St. Read —5E **23**
Rupert Wlk. Read —5E **23**
Ruscombe La. Rusc —5B **16**
Ruscombe Pk. Ind. Est. Rusc
—5B **16**
Ruscombe Rd. Twy —5B **16**
Rushall Clo. Lwr Ear —1F **43**
Rushbrook Rd. Wdly —5B **24**
Rushden Dri. Read —5F **33**
Rushey Way. Lwr Ear —6G **33**
Rushmoor Gdns. Calc —2G **29**
Ruskin Way. Wokgm —2A **46**
Russell Rd. Tok G —3G **11**
Russell St. Read —5A **22**
Russell Way. Winn —5G **35**
Russet Clo. Son C —3D **4**
Russet Glade. Bfld C —6G **39**
Russet Glade. Cav —3D **12**
Rustington Clo. Ear —5A **34**
Rutherford Wlk. Tile —5F **19**
Rutland Rd. Read —5G **21**
Rycroft Clo. Warg —5F **7**
Rydal Av. Tile —2C **20**
Ryecroft Clo. Wdly —3C **24**
Ryeish La. Spen W —5D **42**
Ryhill Way. Lwr Ear —6F **33**
Rylstone Rd. Read —4G **21**

Sackville St. Read —4B **22**
Sadlers Ct. Winn —6A **36**
Sadlers End. Sind —1G **45**
Sadlers La. Winn —6A **36**
Saffron Clo. Ear —2B **34**
Sage Clo. Ear —5H **33**
Sage Rd. Tile —1H **19**
St Andrew's Ct. Read —5E **23**
St Andrew's Hall. Read —6D **12**
St Andrew's Rd. Cav —6A **12**
St Andrews Rd. Hen T —5B **2**

St Annes Clo. Hen T —4C **2**
St Anne's Rd. Cav —2B **22**
St Barnabas Clo. Cav —4B **12**
St Barnabas Rd. Read —5G **33**
St Bartholomews Rd. Read
—5G **23**
St Birinus Rd. Calc —1H **29**
St Catherine's Clo. Sind —5F **35**
St Cecelia Ct. Read —4D **32**
St Clements Clo. Lwr Ear —5B **34**
St David's Clo. Cav —5A **12**
St Edwards Rd. Read —6H **23**
St Elizabeth Clo. Read —1C **42**
St George's Hall. Read —1E **33**
St George's Rd. Read —4E **21**
St George's Ter. Read —4E **21**
St Giles Clo. Read —6C **22**
St Giles Ct. Read —6C 22
(off Southampton St.)
St Helier Clo. Wokgm —5E **47**
St Ives Clo. Thea —4C **28**
St James Clo. Pang —4B **8**
St James Clo. Twy —5B **16**
St Johns Clo. Wdly —4E **25**
St Johns Ga. Read —4C 22
(off Valpy St.)
St John's Hill. Read —5D **22**
St John's Rd. Cav —2D **22**
St John's Rd. Read —5D **22**
St John's St. Read —5D **22**
St Katherine's Rd. Hen T —6C **2**
St Lukes Ct. Cav —6C **12**
St Lukes Way. Cav —6C **12**
St Mark's Clo. Eng —1A **28**
St Mark's Rd. Hen T —5C **2**
St Martin's Cen. Cav —2B **22**
St Martins Clo. Lwr Ear —5B **34**
St Mary's Av. Pur T —5H **9**
St Mary's Butts. Read —5B **22**
St Mary's Clo. Hen T —5A **2**
St Mary's Rd. Sind —6G **35**
St Mary's Way. Bfld C —5G **39**
St Michael's Ct. Rusc —4B **16**
St Michael's Rd. Tile —4A **20**
St Patrick's Av. Charv —5F **15**
St Patrick's Hall. Read —2E **33**
St Paul's Ct. Read —6B **22**
St Paul's Ga. Wokgm —1D **46**
St Peter's Av. Cav —6H **11**
St Peter's Hill. Cav —1A **22**
St Peter's Rd. Read —6H **23**
St Ronan's Rd. Read —4E **21**
St Saviour's Rd. Read —1A **32**
St Saviours Ter. Read —6A **22**
St Stephen's Clo. Cav —2B **22**
St Stephens Ct. Read —5E 23
(off Rupert St.)
St Swithin's Ct. Twy —6A **16**
Salcombe Dri. Ear —2A **34**
Salcombe Rd. Read —3E **33**
Saleby Clo. Lwr Ear —4D **34**
Sale Garden Cotts. Wokgm
—3F **47**
Salford Clo. Read —1D **42**
Salisbury Clo. Wokgm —6D **46**
Salisbury Rd. Read —4H **21**
Salmon Clo. Spen W —6C **42**
Salmond Rd. Read —2D **42**
Saltersgate Clo. Lwr Ear —4C **34**
Sampage Clo. Read —2D **42**
Sanctuary Clo. Tile —4B **20**
Sandcroft Rd. Cav —4H **11**
Sandford Clo. Woodc —2A **49**
Sandford Dri. Wdly —3E **25**
Sandford La. Wdly & Hurst
—5G **25**
Sandgate Av. Tile —2C **20**
Sandhills Way. Calc —2B **30**
Sandleford Clo. Read —2D **42**

Sandown Av. Calc —2G **29**
Sandpit La. D'den —2G **13**
Sandringham Way. Calc —2G **29**
Sandstone Clo. Winn —5H **35**
Sandy La. Wokgm —4H **45**
Sapphire Clo. Wokgm —1B **46**
Sarum Cres. Wokgm —1G **47**
Saturn Clo. Wokgm —2B **46**
Saunders Ct. Pur T —5G **9**
Savernake Clo. Tile —5C **20**
Sawpit Rd. Hurst —5B **26**
Sawtry Clo. Lwr Ear —4D **34**
Saxby Clo. Bfld C —5G **39**
Scafell Clo. Tile —2G **19**
Scarletts La. Kiln G —2E **17**
Scholars Clo. Cav —1A **22**
Schoolfields. S'lake X —1D **14**
School Grn. Shin —4F **43**
School Hill. Warg —1A **16**
School La. Bfld C —5E **39**
School La. Cav —2B **22**
School La. Emm G —5C **12**
School La. Warg —6E **7**
School Rd. Arbor X & B'ham
—6D **44**
School Rd. B'ham —2G **47**
School Rd. Bfld —2H **39**
School Rd. Hurst —5C **26**
School Rd. Tile —4A **20**
School Ter. Read —4F **23**
Scots Dri. Wokgm —6B **36**
Scott Clo. Emm G —5B **12**
Scott Clo. Wdly —5F **25**
Scours La. Tile —3E **21**
Seaford Gdns. Wdly —6D **24**
Seaford Rd. Wokgm —2G **47**
Searles Farm La. Read —5E **31**
Seaton Gdns. Read —4D **32**
Sedgefield Clo. Son C —2E **5**
Sedgewell Rd. Son C —2E **5**
Selborne Ct. Read —5D **22**
Selborne Gdns. Read —3D **20**
Selcourt Clo. Wdly —4C **24**
Sellafield Way. Lwr Ear —4B **34**
Selsdon Av. Wdly —4E **25**
Selsey Way. Lwr Ear —6A **34**
Selva Ct. Read —6D **22**
Send Rd. Cav —2D **22**
Seton Dri. Calc —2C **30**
Settringham Clo. Lwr Ear —4D **34**
Sevenoaks Dri. Spen W —5B **42**
Sevenoaks Rd. Ear —3A **34**
Severn Way. Tile —6C **20**
Sewell Av. Wokgm —6D **36**
Seymour Av. Shin —3F **43**
Shackleton Way. Wdly —5F **25**
Shaftesbury Ct. Wokgm —1G **47**
Shaftesbury Rd. Read —4E **21**
Shakespeare Clo. Cav —1A **22**
Sharnwood Dri. Calc —1C **30**
Sharpethorpe Clo. Lwr Ear
—5A **34**
Shaw Rd. Read —1A **32**
Sheepcot La. Bfld C —6C **40**
Sheep Wlk. Cav —6C **12**
Sheepways La. Tok G —2E **11**
Shefford Cres. Wokgm —6G **37**
Sheldon Gdns. Read —5D **32**
Shelgate Wlk. Wdly —5B **24**
Shelley Clo. Wdly —2D **34**
Shenstone Rd. Read —2C **32**
Shepherd's Av. Ear —4A **24**
Shepherds Hill. Ear —4A **24**
Shepherd's Ho. La. Read —4H **23**
Shepherds La. Cav —4G **11**
Shepherds Wlk. Wdly —4B **24**
Shepherdton La. Graz —6F **41**
Shepley Dri. Read —2F **31**
Sheraton Dri. Tile —3G **19**

Sherbourne Dri. Wdly —4E **25**
Sherfield Clo. Read —2E **33**
Sherfield Dri. Read —2E **33**
Sherfield Hall. Read —2E **33**
Sheridan Av. Cav —5A **12**
Sheridan Way. Wokgm —3B **46**
Sheringham Ct. Read —1D **32**
Sherman Pl. Read —6C **22**
Sherman Rd. Read —6C **22**
Sherwood Gdns. Hen T —5B **2**
Sherwood Pl. Pur T —6G **9**
Sherwood Rise. Pur T —6G **9**
Sherwood Rd. Winn —4H **35**
Sherwood St. Read —1H **33**
Shinfield Ct. Three M —3D **42**
Shinfield Rise. Read —5F **33**
Shinfield Rd. Read —2E **33**
Shiplake Bottom. Pep C —1D **4**
Shiplake Row. S'lake —1B **14**
Shipley Clo. Wdly —3F **25**
Shipton Clo. Tile —2H **19**
Shireshead Clo. Read —6G **21**
Shires, The. Wokgm —4B **46**
Shirley Av. Read —1D **42**
Shirvell's Hill. Woodc —4E **49**
Shoesmiths Ct. Read —4B 22
(off Merchants Pl.)
Shootersbrook La. Uft N —6A **38**
Shooter's Hill. Pang —3A **8**
Shortheath La. Sul'd —5C **38**
Short St. Cav —2C **22**
Short St. Pang —5C **8**
Short St. Read —6C **22**
Short, The. Pur T —5A **10**
Shrubland Dri. Read —2D **30**
Shute End. Wokgm —2E **47**
Sibley Pk. Rd. Ear —4H **33**
Sibson. Lwr Ear —4B **34**
Sidmouth Grange Clo. Ear
—5A **24**
Sidmouth Grange Rd. Ear —5A **24**
Sidmouth St. Read —5D **22**
(in two parts)
Sidney Harrison Ho. Lwr S —5C **6**
Silbury Clo. Calc —2F **29**
Silchester Rd. Read —2F **31**
Silton Clo. Ear —3D **34**
Silver Birches. Wokgm —5H **45**
Silverdale Rd. Ear —3A **34**
Silverdale Rd. Warg —1B **16**
Silver Fox Cres. Wdly —6C **24**
Silver St. Read —6C **22**
Silver St. Flats. Read —6C 22
(off Silver St.)
Silverthorne Dri. Cav —4G **11**
Simmonds St. Read —5B **22**
Simmons Rd. Hen T —2C **2**
Simons Clo. Tile —6H **9**
Simon's La. Wokgm —2H **45**
(in two parts)
Sindlesham Rd. Arbor —5D **44**
Singers Clo. Hen T —5D **2**
Singers La. Hen T —5D **2**
Sirius Clo. Wokgm —2B **46**
Skeffling Clo. Lwr Ear —4D **34**
Skerrit Way. Pur T —6A **10**
Skilton Rd. Tile —1H **19**
Skimerdale Way. Ear —3D **34**
Skye Clo. Calc —2B **30**
Sloane Clo. Gor —5C **48**
Slopes, The. Cav —2E **23**
Smallmead Rd. Read —5G **31**
(in two parts)
Smith Clo. Son C —3E **5**
Smiths Wlk. Wokgm —2C **46**
Snowberry Clo. Wokgm —3C **46**
Snowden Dri. Tile —6F **19**
Snowdrop Gro. Winn —3H **35**
Soham Clo. Lwr Ear —6B **34**

Solent Ct. Read —6C **22**
Somerset Clo. Wokgm —2A **46**
Somerset Wlk. Tile —6G 19
(off Barton Rd.)
Somerstown Ct. Read —5A **22**
Somerton Gdns. Ear —4H **33**
Somerville Clo. Wokgm —4A **46**
Sonning La. Son —2C **24**
Sonning Meadows. Son —3B **24**
Sopwith Clo. Wdly —5F **25**
Sorrel Clo. Bfld C —5G **39**
Sorrel Clo. Wokgm —6H **37**
Southampton St. Read —6C **22**
South Av. Hen T —5D **2**
Southbury La. Rusc —5C **16**
South Clo. Wokgm —2F **47**
(Peach St.)
South Clo. Wokgm —4G **47**
(South Dri.)
Southcote Farm La. Read —1G **31**
Southcote La. Read —2D **30**
Southcote Lodge. Read —2D **30**
Southcote Rd. Read —6G **21**
Southdown Rd. Emm G —5C **12**
South Dri. Read —4D **22**
South Dri. Son —3B **24**
South Dri. Sul'd —1C **38**
South Dri. Wokgm —3F **47**
Southern Ct. Read —5C **22**
Southerndene Clo. Tile —2A **20**
Southern Hill. Read —1E **33**
Southglade. Read —6E **33**
S. Lake Cres. Wdly —1D **34**
Southlands Clo. Wokgm —3G **47**
Southlands Rd. Wokgm —4G **47**
S. Stoke Rd. Woodc —2E **49**
South St. Cav —2C **22**
South St. Read —5C **22**
S. View Av. Cav —2C **22**
Southview Clo. Twy —4B **16**
S. View Pk. Cav —2D **22**
Southwold Clo. Lwr Ear —5C **34**
Southwood. Wokgm —4G **47**
Southwood Gdns. Bfld C —5F **39**
Sovereign Way. Calc —1H **29**
Span Hill. Son —3A **14**
Sparrow Clo. Wokgm —3B **46**
Spencer Clo. Wokgm —2A **46**
Spencer Rd. Read —1C **42**
Spenwood Clo. Spen W —6C **42**
Spey Rd. Tile —5D **20**
Spinney Clo. Emm G —3C **12**
Spinney, The. Calc —2B **30**
Spitfire Way. Wdly —5F **25**
Spode Clo. Tile —4B **20**
Springdale. Ear —4A **34**
Springfield Ct. Twy —5B **16**
Springfield End. Gor —3C **48**
Springfield Pk. Twy —5B **16**
Spring Gdns. Spen W —6C **42**
Spring Gro. Read —6C **22**
Springhill Rd. Gor —3C **48**
Spring La. Son —4A **14**
Spring Ter. Bin H —2H **13**
Spring Ter. Read —1C **32**
Spring Wlk. Warg —6E **7**
Spring Wood La. Bfld C —6F **39**
Springwood La. Roth P —1F **5**
Spruce Rd. Wdly —6F **25**
Spur, The. Warg —5F **7**
Square, The. Ear —6H **33**
Square, The. Spen W —6C **42**
Squirrels Way. Ear —4A **34**
Stable Clo. Bfld C —5F **39**
Staddlestone Clo. Tile —2H **19**
Stadium Way. Tile —3E **21**
Stadium Way Ind. Est. Read
—3E **21**
Stafford Clo. Wdly —4E **25**

A-Z Reading 61

Staffordshire Clo. Read —4C **20**
Stanham Rd. Tile —4C **20**
Stanhope Rd. Read —3E **33**
Stanlake La. Rusc —6C **16**
Stanley Gro. Read —4H **21**
Stanley Rd. Wokgm —2H **47**
Stanley St. Read —4A **22**
Stanshawe Rd. Read —4B **22**
Stanton Clo. Ear —2B **34**
Stanway Cotts. Read —6G **23**
Stapleford Rd. Read —2F **31**
Star La. Read —5C **22**
Starling Clo. Wokgm —3C **46**
Starlings Dri. Tile —1G **29**
Starmead Dri. Wokgm —3G **47**
Star Rd. Cav —2D **22**
Station App. Read —4B **22**
Station Hill. Read —4B **22**
Station Ind. Est. Wokgm —2E **47**
Station Rd. Ear —2B **34**
Station Rd. Gor —5B **48**
Station Rd. Hen T —4D **2**
Station Rd. Lwr S —4B **6**
Station Rd. Pang —4B **8**
Station Rd. Read —4B **22**
Station Rd. Thea —3D **28**
Station Rd. Twy —6A **16**
Station Rd. Warg —1H **15**
Station Rd. Wokgm —2E **47**
Staverton Clo. Wokgm —2H **47**
Staverton Rd. Read —3D **32**
Steeple Wlk. Lwr Ear —6G **33**
Stephanie Chase Ct. Wokgm
—1G **47**
Stephen Clo. Twy —1C **26**
Sterling Way. Read —3D **20**
Stirling Clo. Cav —4E **13**
Stockbury Clo. Ear —5A **34**
Stockton Rd. Read —5C **32**
Stoke Ct. Read —5C **32**
Stoke Row Rd. Roth P —1D **4**
Stokes View. Pang —5B **8**
Stonea Clo. Lwr Ear —6B **34**
Stoneham Clo. Tile —6D **20**
Stonehaven Dri. Wdly —6F **25**
Stone St. Read —3E **21**
Stour Clo. Tile —4D **20**
Stowe Clo. Lwr Ear —4C **34**
Stowmarket Clo. Lwr Ear —4C **34**
Straight Mile, The. Shur R &
Wokgm —3G **27**
Strand Way. Lwr Ear —5A **34**
Stratford Way. Read —5B **22**
Strathdean Pl. Read —4A **22**
Strathmore Dri. Charv —6F **15**
Strathy Clo. Read —4E **21**
Stratton Gdns. Read —5D **32**
Street, The. Eng —1A **28**
Street, The. Tid —2C **18**
Stuart Clo. Emm G —5C **12**
Studland Clo. Read —1D **42**
Sturbridge Clo. Lwr Ear —5B **34**
Sturges Rd. Wokgm —3F **47**
Suffolk Clo. Wokgm —2A **46**
Suffolk Rd. Read —5G **21**
Sulham Hill. Sul —3D **18**
Sulham La. Sul —1D **18**
Sulhamstead Hill. Sul'd —2B **38**
Sulhamstead Rd. Sul'd —4C **38**
Sulhamstead Rd. Uft N —4F **39**
Sulham Wlk. Read —2E **31**
Summerfield Clo. Wokgm —5C **36**
Summerfield Rise. Gor —4D **48**
Sunderland Clo. Wdly —4G **25**
Sundew Clo. Wokgm —6H **37**
Sun Gdns. Bfld C —6F **39**
Sun St. Read —5E **23**
Surley Row. Cav —4B **12**
(in three parts)

Surrey Rd. Read —2C **32**
Sussex Gdns. Wdly —5D **24**
Sussex La. Spen W —6D **42**
Sutcliffe Av. Ear —2C **34**
Sutherland Gro. Calc —2B **30**
Sutherlands Av. Read —1D **32**
Suttons Bus. Pk. Read —4G **23**
Suttons Pk. Av. Read —4F **23**
Sutton Wlk. Read —1D **32**
Swainstone Rd. Read —1C **32**
Swallow Clo. Tile —6H **19**
Swallowfield Dri. Read —2C **42**
Swallowfield Gdns. Thea —2D **28**
Swallowfield Rd. Arbor —6B **44**
Swallow Way. Wokgm —3B **46**
Swanholm Gdns. Calc —2C **30**
Swanmore Clo. Lwr Ear —5D **34**
Swan Pl. Read —5B **22**
Swans Ct. Twy —1B **26**
Swansea Cotts. Tile —3B **20**
Swansea Rd. Read —3B **22**
Swansea Ter. Tile —3B **20**
Swanston Field. Whit T —3C **8**
Sweet Briar Dri. Calc —2H **29**
Swepstone Clo. Lwr Ear —4B **34**
Swift Clo. Wokgm —3B **46**
Swinbrook Clo. Tile —1A **20**
Swing Brook Clo. Tile —1A **20**
Swiss Cotts. Clo. Tile —4H **19**
Swiss Farm Caravan Site. Hen T
—1C **2**
Sycamore Clo. Bfld —3G **39**
Sycamore Clo. Wdly —1B **34**
Sycamore Ct. Pang —4B **8**
Sycamore Dri. Twy —5A **16**
Sycamore Rd. Read —4F **33**
Sylvan Wlk. Read —2F **31**

Tadcroft Wlk. Calc —3B **30**
Taff Way. Tile —5D **20**
Tagg La. D'den —2G **13**
Tag La. Hare H —1D **16**
Talbot Clo. Cav —2E **23**
Talbot Ct. Read —5B **22**
Talbot Way. Tile —1H **19**
Talfourd Av. Read —1H **33**
Tallis La. Read —2G **31**
Tamar Gdns. Read —3D **32**
Tamarind Way. Ear —5G **33**
Tamarisk Av. Read —5F **33**
Tamarisk Rise. Wokgm —1F **47**
Tamar Way. Wokgm —2B **46**
Tamworth Clo. Lwr Ear —5B **34**
Tanfield. Read —3D **32**
Tangley Dri. Wokgm —4E **47**
Tanhouse La. Wokgm —3D **46**
Tanners Clo. Bfld C —6E **39**
Tanners La. Chalk —2A **12**
Tape La. Hurst —4C **26**
Targett Ct. Winn —4G **35**
Tarlton Ct. Tile —6C **20**
Tarragon Clo. Ear —5G **33**
Tarragon Way. Bfld C —5G **39**
Tattersall Clo. Wokgm —3H **47**
Tavistock Rd. Read —3C **32**
Taylor Ct. Read —1H **33**
Taynton Wlk. Read —1C **32**
Tay Rd. Tile —4D **20**
Tazewell Ct. Read —6A **22**
Technology Cen. Thea —4D **28**
Telford Cres. Wdly —3E **25**
Temple M. Wdly —5E **25**
Temple Pl. Read —6B **22**
Templeton Gdns. Read —5D **32**
Tenby Av. Cav —5E **13**
Tennyson Rd. Wdly —2D **34**
Tern Clo. Tile —5D **20**
Terrace, The. Wokgm —2E **47**

Tessa Rd. Read —3A **22**
Test Clo. Tile —4D **20**
Tetbury Ct. Read —5H **21**
Teviot Rd. Tile —5B **20**
Thames Av. Pang —4C **8**
Thames Av. Read —3B **22**
Thames Bank S. Whit T —3C **8**
Thames Dri. Charv —4E **15**
Thames Reach. Pur T —6A **10**
Thames Rd. Gor —5B **48**
Thames Side. Hen T —3D **2**
(in two parts)
Thames Side. Read —3B **22**
(in two parts)
Thames Side Promenade. Read
—2A **22**
Thames St. Son —6C **14**
Thames Ter. Son —6C **14**
Thames Valley Bus. Pk. Cav
—3H **23**
Thames Valley Pk. Dri. Cav
—4G **23**
Thanington Way. Lwr Ear —4A **34**
Thanksgiving La. Bin H —1G **13**
Theale Commercial Est. Thea
—3E **29**
Theale Rd. Bfld —1G **39**
Theobald Dri. Tile —6A **10**
Thetford M. Cav —4E **13**
Thicket Rd. Tile —4B **20**
Thirlmere Av. Tile —2C **20**
Thistledown. Tile —3H **19**
Thistleton Way. Lwr Ear —4D **34**
Thomson Wlk. Calc —2B **30**
Thornbers Way. Charv —5G **15**
Thornbridge Rd. Read —6C **32**
Thornbury Grn. Twy —5A **16**
Thorney Clo. Lwr Ear —4D **34**
Thorn La. Read —5C **22**
Thorn St. Read —5B **22**
Thornton M. Read —4G **21**
Thornton Rd. Read —4G **21**
Thorn Wlk. Read —4A **22**
(off Weldale St.)
Thorpe Clo. Wokgm —5D **46**
Thrale M. Read —4E **21**
Three Gables La. Stread —4A **48**
Thrush Clo. Bfld C —5G **39**
Thurlestone Gdns. Read —4D **32**
Thurnscoe Clo. Lwr Ear —6G **33**
Thurso Clo. Tile —4D **20**
Thyme Clo. Ear —5G **33**
Tickhill Clo. Lwr Ear —1G **43**
Tidmarsh La. Tid —2A **18**
Tidmarsh Rd. Pang —1C **18**
Tidmarsh St. Read —3E **21**
Tidmore La. Woodc —2G **49**
Tiffany Clo. Wokgm —2A **46**
Tiger Clo. Wdly —5G **25**
Tigerseye Clo. Wokgm —1A **46**
Tilbury Clo. Cav —1D **22**
Tilebarn Clo. Hen T —4B **2**
Tilebarn La. Hen T —4B **2**
Tilehurst Rd. Read —6E **21**
Tilling Clo. Tile —2G **19**
Tilney Way. Lwr Ear —6G **33**
Tinsley Clo. Lwr Ear —6G **33**
Tintern Cres. Read —1A **32**
Tippett Rise. Read —1C **32**
Tippings La. Wdly —3F **25**
Tithebarn Gro. Calc —2C **30**
Tiverton Clo. Wdly —3D **24**
Tiwell Clo. Lwr Ear —4D **34**
Tofrek Ter. Read —5F **21**
Tokersgreen La. Kid E —3G **11**
Tokers Grn. Rd. Tok G —1G **11**
Topaz Clo. Wokgm —1B **46**
Torcross Gro. Calc —2G **29**
Torrington Rd. Read —4D **32**

Toseland Way. Lwr Ear —3D **34**
Totnes Rd. Read —4D **32**
Totterdown. Bfld C —6E **39**
Toutley Clo. Wokgm —5B **36**
Toutley Rd. Wokgm —4C **36**
Tower Clo. Cav —2D **12**
Town Pl. Read —5E **23**
Townsend Rd. Streat —4A **48**
Trafalgar Clo. Wokgm —2B **46**
Trafalgar Ct. Read —6G **21**
Trafalgar Ho. Read —3A **22**
Trafford Rd. Read —3H **21**
Treacher Ct. Twy —5B **16**
Tredegar Rd. Cav —5A **12**
Tree Clo. Tile —4A **20**
Trefoil Clo. Wokgm —1H **47**
Treforgan. Cav —5A **12**
Trelawney Dri. Tile —3G **19**
Trelleck Rd. Read —1A **32**
Trent Clo. Wokgm —1B **46**
Trenthams Clo. Pur T —5G **9**
Treyarnon Ct. Read —6F **23**
Triangle, The. Tile —4A **20**
Tring Rd. Tile —1H **19**
Trinity Clo. Hen T —4C **2**
Trinity Ct. Wokgm —1C **46**
Trinity Pl. Read —5A **22**
Triptree Clo. Lwr Ear —6G **33**
Troon Ct. Read —5E **23**
Troutbeck Clo. Twy —4A **16**
Trust Corner. Hen T —5D **2**
Trusthorpe Clo. Lwr Ear —4D **34**
Tudor Clo. Wokgm —3H **47**
Tudor Rd. Read —4B **22**
Tuns Hill Cotts. Read —1H **33**
Tuns La. Hen T —3D **2**
Tupsley Rd. Read —1A **32**
Turmeric Clo. Ear —5G **33**
Turnberry Ct. Read —5E **23**
(off Muirfield Clo.)
Turnbridge Clo. Lwr Ear —6A **34**
Turnstone Clo. Winn —3G **35**
Tuscan Clo. Tile —3B **20**
Tuxford M. Read —5E **23**
Tweed Ct. Tile —5E **21**
Twin Oaks. Emm G —4C **12**
Two Tree Hill. Hen T —5A **2**
Twyford Rd. Binf —6E **37**
Twyford Rd. Twy —3A **16**
Twyford Rd. Wokgm —6E **37**
Tyberton Pl. Read —1A **32**
Tyler Clo. Cav —5H **11**
Tyle Rd. Tile —4A **20**
Tylers Pl. Tile —4C **20**
Tylorstown. Cav —5A **12**
Tyrrel Ct. Read —5D **22**

Uffington Clo. Tile —4H **19**
Uffoot Clo. Lwr Ear —6G **33**
Ullswater Dri. Tile —1A **20**
Ulster Clo. Cav —5E **13**
Uncles La. Wal L —1H **27**
Underwood Rd. Read —2C **30**
Union St. Read —4B **22**
Unity Clo. Emm G —5C **12**
Unity Ct. Emm G —5C **12**
Upavon Dri. Read —1H **31**
Uplands Rd. Cav —5H **11**
Up. Crown St. Read —6C **22**
Up. Culham Rd. C Grn —3H **3**
Up. Meadow Rd. Read —4E **33**
Up. Red Cross Rd. Gor —5C **48**
Up. Redlands Rd. Read —1E **33**
Up. Warren Av. Cav —1F **21**
Up. Woodcote Rd. Cav —5G **11**
Uppingham Dri. Wdly —3E **25**
Uppingham Gdns. Cav —4E **13**
Upton Clo. Hen T —4D **2**

Upton Rd. Tile —5E 21
Usk Rd. Tile —6C 20

Vachel Rd. Read —4B 22
Vale Cres. Tile —3B 20
Valentia Clo. Read —4G 21
Valentia Rd. Read —4G 21
Valentine Clo. Read —5G 33
Valentine Cres. Cav —6D 12
Valerie Ct. Read —6H 21
Valley Clo. Cav —6B 12
Valley Clo. Gor —5C 48
Valley Cres. Wokgm —6D 36
Valley Rd. Bfld C —5F 39
Valley Rd. Hen T —5A 2
Valpy St. Read —4C 22
Vanbrugh Ct. Read —5E 23
Vanlore Way. Calc —1H 29
Vastern Ct. Read —3B 22
Vastern Rd. Read —3B 22
Vauxhall Dri. Wdly —6E 25
Venetia Clo. Cav —3D 12
Ventnor Rd. Tile —4A 20
Venus Clo. Wokgm —2C 46
Verbena Clo. Winn —3F 35
Verey Clo. Twy —1C 26
Verney M. Read —5F 21
Vernon Cres. Read —1C 42
Vicarage Rd. Hen T —4D 2
Vicarage Rd. Read —1D 32
Vicarage Wood. Tile —2G 19
Vickers Clo. Shin —4G 43
Vickers Clo. Wdly —6G 25
Victoria Ct. Hen T —4D 2
Victoria M. Read —3G 21
Victoria Rd. Cav —1B 22
Victoria Rd. Tile —4A 20
Victoria Rd. Warg —6F 7
Victoria Sq. Read —5E 23
Victoria St. Read —5E 23
Victoria Way. Read —5E 23
Victor Way. Wdly —5F 25
Village Clo. Read —2C 42
Villa M. Read —5F 23
Villiers Mead. Wokgm —2D 46
Vincent Clo. Wdly —6E 25
Vine Cres. Read —2D 30
Vinery, The. Warg —6E 7
Vines, The. Wokgm —5H 45
Virginia Way. Read —2E 31
Viscount Way. Wdly —5E 25
Voller Dri. Tile —6H 19
Volunteer Rd. Thea —4C 28
Vulcan Clo. Wdly —3G 25

Wagtail Clo. Twy —6B 16
Waingels Rd. Land E —3F 25
Waldeck St. Read —1C 32
Walden Av. Arbor —5B 44
Waleys Pl. Cav —2D 22
Walkers Pl. Read —5F 21
Wallace Clo. Wdly —1C 24
Walled Gdns. Warg —6E 7
Wallingford Rd. Gor & N Sto
—5C 48
Wallingford Rd. Streat & Moul
—5A 48
Wallner Way. Wokgm —3H 47
Walmer Clo. Tile —6D 20
Walmer Rd. Wdly —3E 25
Walnut Clo. Wokgm —3C 46
Walnut Tree Clo. Rusc —4B 16
Walnut Tree Ct. Gor —5C 48
Walnut Way. Tile —4A 20
Walrus Clo. Wdly —5G 25
Walter Rd. Wokgm —6B 36
Waltham Ct. Gor —3C 48

Waltham Rd. Rusc —5C 16
Waltham Rd. Twy —6A 16
Walton Av. Hen T —5D 2
Walton Clo. Wdly —5B 24
Wandhope Way. Tile —2H 19
Wantage Hall. Read —1E 33
Wantage Rd. Read —5F 21
Wantage Rd. Streat —3A 48
Warbler Clo. Tile —6G 19
Warborough Av. Tile —5G 19
Warbreck Dri. Tile —1G 19
Ward Clo. Wokgm —6G 37
Wardle Av. Tile —3A 20
Wargrave Hill. Warg —6E 7
Wargrave Rd. Hen T & Lwr S
—4E 3
Wargrave Rd. Twy —3A 16
Waring Clo. Lwr Ear —6B 34
Warley Rise. Tile —6G 9
War Memorial Pl. Hen T —6D 2
Warnford Rd. Tile —5C 20
Warnsham Clo. Lwr Ear —5A 34
Warren Clo. Bfld C —5F 39
Warren Ct. Cav —2A 22
Warren Ho. Rd. Wokgm —4G 37
Warren Rd. Son & Wdly —3C 24
Warren Row Rd. Know H —1H 7
Warren, The. Cav —1G 21
Warwick Rd. Read —2D 32
Washington Rd. Cav —2C 22
Waterford Way. Wokgm —2F 47
Waterloo Clo. Wokgm —3H 47
Waterloo Cres. Wokgm —3H 47
Waterloo Rise. Read —2C 32
Waterloo Rd. Read —1C 32
Waterloo Rd. Wokgm —3H 47
Waterman Pl. Read —3B 22
Watermans Rd. Hen T —5D 2
Waterman's Way. Warg —1H 15
Water Rd. Read —5E 21
Watersfield Clo. Lwr Ear —6H 33
Waterside Dri. Pur T —5A 10
Waterside Dri. Thea —3E 29
Waterside Gdns. Read —5B 22
Watlington St. Read —5D 22
(in two parts)
Watmore La. Winn —3A 36
Wavell Clo. Read —5G 33
Waverley Ct. Read —6G 21
(off Southcote Rd.)
Waverley Rd. Read —4E 21
Waverley Way. Wokgm —6C 46
Waybrook Cres. Read —6G 23
Waylen St. Read —5A 22
Wayside Grn. Woodc —2F 49
Wealden Way. Tile —3B 20
Weald Rise. Tile —2C 20
Webb St. Wokgm —6H 37
Wedderburn Clo. Winn —4A 36
Wedgewood Way. Tile —3C 20
Weighbridge Row. Read —3A 22
Weir Clo. Calc —2C 30
Weirside Ct. Read —5E 23
Welby Cres. Winn —5G 35
Weldale St. Read —4A 22
Welford Rd. Wdly —4F 25
Welland Clo. Tile —3H 19
Wellfield Clo. Tile —5H 19
Wellington Av. Read —2E 33
Wellington St. Spen W —5B 42
Wellington Ind. Est. Spen W
—6B 42
Wellington Rd. Wokgm —2E 47
Wells Hall. Read —1E 33
Welwick Clo. Lwr Ear —4D 34
Wendover Way. Tile —5A 20
Wenlock Edge. Charv —6G 15
Wensley Clo. Twy —5A 16
Wensley Rd. Read —2G 31

Wentworth Av. Read —6E 33
Wescott Rd. Wokgm —2G 47
Wesley Ga. Read —5D 22
Wessex Gdns. Twy —1B 26
Wessex Hall. Read —1G 33
Westbourne Ter. Read —5F 21
Westbrook Rd. Read —3F 21
Westbury La. Pur T —4F 9
W. Chiltern. Woodc —3F 49
Westcote Rd. Read —6G 21
Westcott Rd. Wokgm —2G 47
Westdene Cres. Cav —6H 11
West Dri. Calc —1B 30
West Dri. Son —3C 24
Westerham Wlk. Read —1C 32
(off Charndon Clo.)
Western Av. Hen T —5D 2
Western Av. Wdly —4C 24
Western Elms Av. Read —5H 21
Western Oaks. Tile —2B 20
Western Rd. Hen T —5D 2
Western Rd. Read —6H 21
Westfield Cres. S'lake —5C 6
Westfield Rd. Cav —2C 22
Westfield Rd. Winn —4G 35
West Grn. Ct. Read —1A 32
West Hill. Read —6C 22
Westlands Av. Read —5F 33
Westleigh Dri. Son C —4E 5
Westminster Way. Lwr Ear
—5B 34
Westmorland Clo. Wokgm —2A 46
Westonbirt Dri. Cav —1H 21
Westridge Av. Pur T —5H 9
West St. Hen T —3C 2
West St. Read —5B 22
Westview Dri. Twy —4B 16
Westward Rd. Wokgm —1C 46
Westway. Gor —3C 48
Westwood Glen. Tile —4H 19
Westwood Rd. Tile —3A 20
Westwood Row. Tile —2H 19
Wetherby Clo. Cav —4D 12
Whaley Rd. Wokgm —6G 37
Wharfdale Rd. Winn —3F 35
Wharfe La. Hen T —3D 2
Wharf, The. Pang —4B 8
Wheatfields Rd. Shin —3F 43
Wheatlands Clo. Calc —2B 30
Wheatley Clo. Read —5F 33
Wheble Dri. Wdly —4C 24
Wheeler Clo. Bfld C —5G 39
Wheelton Clo. Ear —4H 33
Whitamore Row. Hen T —5D 2
(off Trust Corner)
Whitby Clo. Cav —5E 13
Whitby Dri. Read —1D 32
Whitby Grn. Cav —4E 13
Whitchurch Rd. Pang —4C 8
Whitebeam Clo. Wokgm —5A 46
Whitegates La. Ear —5H 23
Whitehart Clo. Thea —2D 28
White Hill. Hen T —3E 3
Whitehills Grn. Gor —5C 48
Whitehouse Rd. Woodc —3F 49
Whiteknights Hall. Read —1F 33
Whiteknights Rd. Read —1G 33
White Lodge Clo. Tile —1G 19
White's Hill. Sul'd —3C 38
Whitestone Clo. Lwr Ear —3D 34
Whitewell Clo. Arbor X —6D 44
Whitley Pk. Farm Ho. Read —2D 32
Whitley Pk. La. Read —2E 33
Whitley St. Read —1C 32
Whitley Wood La. Read —1C 42
(in two parts)
Whitley Wood Rd. Read —2C 42
Whitstone Gdns. Read —5D 32
Whitton Clo. Lwr Ear —5C 34

Wickford Way. Lwr Ear —6G 33
Wickham Rd. Lwr Ear —5D 34
Wicks La. Shur R —2H 27
Widecombe Pl. Read —5C 32
Widmore La. Son C —3F 5
Wield Clo. Lwr Ear —5D 34
Wigmore La. Read —3E 21
(in two parts)
Wigmore La. Thea —4B 28
Wild Clo. Lwr Ear —6B 34
Wildcroft Dri. Wokgm —6D 46
Wilder Av. Pang —5D 8
Wilderness Ct. Ear —3H 33
Wilderness Rd. Ear —4G 33
William St. Read —4A 22
Willow Clo. Bfld —3G 39
Willow Dri. Twy —4A 16
Willow Gdns. Read —5F 33
Willow Gdns. Tile —2G 19
Willowherb Clo. Wokgm —1H 47
Willow La. Warg —4D 6
Willowside. Wdly —3E 25
Willows, The. Cav —2B 22
Willow St. Read —6B 22
Willow Tree Glade. Calc —2H 29
Wilmington Clo. Wdly —4E 25
Wilmott Clo. Winn —6G 35
Wilsford Clo. Lwr Ear —1F 43
Wilson Av. Hen T —5D 2
Wilson Ct. Winn —6G 35
Wilson Rd. Read —5F 21
Wilton Ho. Read —6G 21
Wilton Rd. Read —4F 21
Wiltshire Dri. Wokgm —1G 47
Wiltshire Rd. Wokgm —6F 37
Wiltshire Wlk. Tile —6G 19
Wilwyne Clo. Cav —6D 12
Wimblington Dri. Lwr Ear —6B 34
Wimborne Gdns. Tile —3D 20
Wincanton Rd. Read —1D 42
Winchcombe Rd. Twy —1B 26
Winchester Rd. Cav —2C 22
Wincroft Rd. Cav —5H 11
Windermere Clo. Winn —3H 35
Windermere Rd. Read —3E 33
Windmill Av. Wokgm —6B 36
Windmill Clo. Wokgm —6B 36
Windrush Ct. Read —5E 21
Windrush Way. Read —5E 21
Windsor Ct. Read —5H 21
Windsor Hall. Read —1F 33
Windsor Sq. Read —6C 22
Windsor Way. Calc —2G 29
Wingate Rd. Wdly —6D 24
Wingrove Rd. Read —6F 21
Winkfield Clo. Wokgm —5E 47
Winnersh Ga. Winn —4A 36
Winnersh Gro. Winn —5H 35
Winnersh Triangle Ind. Est. Winn
—3G 35
Winser Dri. Read —2G 31
Winston Clo. Spen W —6E 43
Winston Way. Pur T —5G 9
Winterberry Way. Cav —4H 11
Winton Rd. Read —6E 33
Wintringham Way. Pur T —5A 10
Wise's Firs. Sul'd —5C 38
Wispington Clo. Lwr Ear —4C 34
Wisteria Clo. Wokgm —3C 46
Wiston Ter. Read —4C 22
Witcham Clo. Lwr Ear —6C 34
Withy Clo. Tile —1H 29
Wittenham Av. Tile —4G 19
Wittenham Clo. Woodc —3G 49
Woburn Clo. Cav —4H 11
Wokingham Rd. Hurst —4C 26
Wokingham Rd. Read —5F 23
Wolseley St. Read —2B 22
Wolsey Ho. Gor —5C 48